Storytellers' True Stories of Triumph

Edited by

Anne E. Beall, PhD & Judi Lee
Goshen

Chicago Story Press, Inc.

STORYTELLERS' TRUE STORIES OF TRIUMPH

Cover Designed by Atiq Ahmed.
Image licensed through 123rf.com/free images/Virtosmedia
© <a href='https://www.123rf.com/profile_virtosmedia'>virtosmedia</a>, <a href='https://www.123rf.com/free-images/'>123RF Free Images</a>

ISBN: 979-8-9874649-2-2 (Paperback)
ISBN: 979-8-9874649-3-9 (Hard Cover)

This book is dedicated to all those facing adversity around the world. Your resilience is a reminder of the strength of the human spirit.

Hang in there–your story of triumph is yet to be told.

*And in loving memory of **Jonathan Euseppi**, whose remarkable optimism and courage will always inspire us.*

Table of Contents

Introduction: Embracing Triumph Over Adversity

In the grand tapestry of human existence, life is a series of unpredictable twists and turns. It often throws us curveballs that we could never have anticipated, testing not only our character but the very essence of who we are. These are moments when we come face to face with hardship, a formidable enemy that knows no prejudice. It strikes without warning, targeting our health, our dreams, and our sense of self.

But adversity, for all its cruelty, also possesses a profound capacity for transformation. It is within this hardship that we discover our truest selves, finding reserves of strength we never knew existed, unraveling hidden potential, and, most importantly, learning to triumph over the darkest times in life.

The stories within these pages are a testament to the extraordinary power of the human spirit. They are the chronicles of individuals who have journeyed through the storms of life, facing down illness, infertility, loss, and violence. Each storyteller follows their own unique path, confronting a distinct set of challenges, yet they share a common thread—the unwavering determination to keep going and eventually triumph.

Many of these narratives are deeply rooted in health issues—a harrowing journey of overcoming a heart attack, enduring intense pain initially disregarded by physicians, surviving multiple strokes, and teetering on the brink of death. For some, the battle was against a relentless illness that threatened to consume them. These courageous people navigated hospitals, endured surgeries, and wrestled with the anguish of uncertain outcomes. But, in the end, they discovered the resilience to prevail. One woman's story takes us on an extraordinary journey as she came so close to death that she had a profound visit with the afterlife.

Some stories delve into the realm of childhood experiences. One features a young girl left alone in a school building on a snowy day. She's afraid, but she figures out how to handle the situation, showing the bravery kids can have when adults let them down. Another tells of a child, just five years old, who had to take care of her mother with special needs. This narrative highlights the strength and love children can show under tough circumstances.

We also have an author who had a dangerous childhood accident, nearly biting off her tongue. She eventually recovered and found her voice again, illustrating how children can overcome serious challenges and grow from them.

One young man yearned for a dream that seemed beyond his reach—to attend Northwestern University and study English. His father stood in opposition, refusing to co-sign a loan, a formidable barrier to his aspirations. But he didn't surrender his dreams to circumstance. Through determination, hard work, and a belief in himself, he obtained his dream and ultimately became an English teacher. His story shows how determination can shape a life.

Others grappled with the heart-wrenching struggle to conceive a child, a dream that seemed perpetually out of reach. Their narratives show the power of hope and the enduring love that fuels the human spirit. Through the trials of fertility treatments and the rollercoaster of emotions, they eventually brought life into the world.

In the face of a terminal cancer diagnosis, one couple found a profound understanding of the finite nature of life. Instead of surrendering to despair, they embarked on a journey to live each day to its fullest, savoring the beauty of existence with newfound intensity. Their history is a lesson in the art of embracing every moment.

Loss, too, is an inevitable part of life's journey. One storyteller recounted the painful unraveling of her career, a source of fulfillment and purpose. She navigated unemployment, rediscovering her identity and forging a new path. She reminds us that even when the job we cherish slips through our fingers, the essence of our worth can remain intact.

Among these tales, one woman learned after decades that her husband was not the person she knew, which made her question her marriage. She eventually realized that she had to be true to herself and leave a long-term relationship behind. Her journey toward self-discovery and the courage to walk a different path demonstrates the strength it takes to reinvent one's life at any age, even when it means letting go of the familiar.

Another woman embarked on a daring adventure to Rome, a city where she knew neither the language nor the culture. Her initial days were fraught with harassment and the threat of danger. Yet, in the face of hardship, she found work and, more importantly, discovered true independence. Through many lonely months, she built a fulfilling life in a city she initially didn't understand, proving that pursuing one's dreams can lead to unexpected triumphs.

Yet another individual found herself in the terrible position of being a doctoral student for a professor who treated her like a domestic worker. Initially, she complied with demeaning tasks such as cleaning her graduate advisor's home. However, she came to realize that self-respect is worth more than any degree. Her triumph is remarkable because she almost paid the ultimate price for her refusal and nearly didn't obtain her doctorate. Her unwavering stand for dignity and self-worth is remarkable.

In addition to these incredible stories, this anthology features narratives of those who fought and conquered alcoholism, who faced having their children taken away by a vengeful spouse, and who found themselves on a date with someone on a suicide mission.

All these storytellers conquered their foes and went on to live fulfilling lives despite what they experienced.

For one author, growing up in an abusive household led to a lifetime of overcoming that ultimately led them to claim a new name and live a life of authenticity as a transgender individual. Another person escaped the shackles of a toxic corporate job, summoning the courage to leave it all behind to pursue a lifelong dream— professional roller skating!

Among these tales, one story stands as a harrowing reminder of the darkness that can infiltrate our lives. A victim of domestic violence shares her story, a painful odyssey of courage and survival. Her narrative serves as a stark reminder that triumph can take many forms, sometimes as simple as breaking free from a relationship that binds us.

Depression, a relentless adversary of the mind, cast its shadow over many of these storytellers. Yet, through support and sheer determination, these individuals clawed their way back to the light. They remind us that, even in the depths of despair, there is hope, and the capacity to heal is within us all.

When I read these stories, I noticed that adversity didn't come gradually; it hit people like a speeding train. Every person faced moments of despair, wondering if they could ever overcome their ordeal. Despite these doubts, they persisted, repeatedly picking themselves up and trying again. It wasn't always certain that they would ultimately succeed, but they persevered. At times, they surprised themselves by triumphing over their tragedies. Their resilience gives me hope.

In the following chapters, you will immerse yourself in the lives of these remarkable individuals. Each one shows the strength of the human spirit, and the victory that can arise from the most challenging of circumstances. These tales are more than inspiring; they are a profound education in facing difficulties head-on.

As you read these stories, my wish is that you find inspiration, hope, and the belief that within you, too, lies the power to triumph over any obstacle that life may present. These storytellers have shown us the way. Now, let their tales light your path as well.

Anne E. Beall, Ph.D.

1 | It Could Happen to You by Toneal M. Jackson

Who knew that a twenty-four-year-old could have a stroke?

Not me. And I was the one it happened to. I'll never forget that day.

I'd come home from work after dealing with a migraine during my entire shift. I found a quiet room, closed the door, turned off the lights, and laid in complete darkness until I drifted off to sleep. When I woke up, I realized the lateness of the hour and encouraged myself to start dinner. Not fully recovered from the headache, I gathered enough strength to make some fish and rice. My daughters weren't home, so I made my husband's plate and brought it to him. I then fixed my plate and joined him on the couch in the living room. The next thing I knew, I felt a weird tingly sensation in my arm.

"Something's wrong with my arm, Jerome. Take my plate." I managed to utter before my entire right side went totally numb.

My face froze, and I was unable to move for a few minutes. Then, it seemed as though whatever this was had passed.

My husband just stared at me and said I needed to go to the hospital. I tried my best to assure him I was fine. I didn't know what happened, but it was over. I felt fine, so there was no need to make a big deal out of it. I went upstairs.

A few minutes later, I heard him say, "Get the phone."

"Get the phone?" I thought to myself. I didn't even hear it ring. I picked up the phone, and my dad was on the other end.

Did he really just tell on me? I thought to myself. I couldn't believe this.

"My son told me you just had some kind of episode."

"Yeah," was all I could mumble, still in disbelief that my husband called my dad to tell on me. I felt like a ten-year-old being fussed at for something I'd done wrong.

"I think you should go to the hospital," he continued.

"But Dad, I'm fine. Jerome is just blowing things out of proportion. I'll lay down for a little while and I'm sure I'll be fine."

"Toneal ..." He said in a disapproving tone.

"Dad."

"If you won't do it for yourself, do it for him. That way he won't worry," he bargained.

"If I go, will you leave me alone?"

"Yes. Do it for me AND my son."

You would've thought that it was actually his son, the allegiance he had with my husband. I began preparing myself for what I knew was a pointless trip.

"Now, I have to sit at the hospital all night in this ER—like I have nothing better to do with my time," I complained.

He better be glad I don't want to hear my dad's mouth. The nerve of him. I can't believe he told on me. I continued in my mind.

Jerome was waiting by the door. We got in the car and headed to the hospital. As we pulled up to the emergency room entrance, he asked if I wanted to get out while he parked. I told him it wasn't necessary. As we were walking through the parking lot, he kept asking if I was okay.

"Jerome, I'm fine. Please don't ask me a—"

Before I could finish my sentence, I passed out. Right in the middle of the parking lot. Legs gave out and I fell, unable to move. When I regained consciousness, I was in the ER on a stretcher; this time my speech was totally slurred. The nurse asked if I could tell her what happened, and I gave as many details as I could recall. Because of the symptoms I presented—headache, tingling in my arms, temporary paralysis, slurring of speech—she said they needed to do a CT scan.

Apparently, they didn't like what they saw because the next words I heard were, "We have to admit you."

I couldn't argue because my head was spinning and my speech was extremely slurred, and no one would have understood me anyway, so I silently agreed.

The doctor later explained the CT scan revealed multiple spots on my brain, which caused concern. They wanted to monitor me and run more tests, including an MRI. Now, if you've never had an MRI done, let's just say it's not for the faint at heart. It's most comparable to being buried alive. I was inside an especially tight space and told I could not move for forty-five minutes. I tried my best not to focus on my claustrophobia, however, the time was not ticking by fast enough.

Once the test was finally over, I went back to my room. A couple of hours later, the doctors came inside and said that they still couldn't release me. Based upon my results, they thought I might have multiple sclerosis, so they wanted to conduct further tests. My speech was still slurred, and I could not walk on my own, so, again, I silently agreed.

A few days, and a gamut of MRIs, EKGs, and EEGs (tests that monitor the heart and brain), I learned that I'd suffered a stroke, but they couldn't identify a cause. I was instructed to undergo physical therapy and assigned to a neurologist. I left that hospital feeling like a complete and utter failure.

As an overachiever and perfectionist, without an explanation of what caused this stroke, I immediately believed it was my fault. I felt ashamed and embarrassed because I was a few weeks away from my twenty-fifth birthday, and I couldn't walk by myself or talk without someone asking me to repeat what I'd said. My speech was that slurred.

I started slipping into a depression. What was wrong with me? Why couldn't I just talk? Why couldn't I just go back to being my normal self? It had been over a week, and I wasn't improving.

I wish I could've explained to my twenty-five-year-old self that I needed to learn patience. I needed to set aside unrealistic expectations and give myself some grace. It was okay to be down. It wasn't my fault I had a stroke. Statistically speaking, it wasn't far-fetched that it happened to me.

I learned women are more likely to have strokes than men. Blacks are more susceptible to have strokes than their counterparts. If someone in your immediate family had a stroke, it's very possible that it could happen to you.

Well, here I was a black woman whose biological father died from a stroke, so I was the perfect "candidate." But it took years before I'd put those puzzle pieces together.

A few months after my stroke, I began to recover. My strength returned along with my speech. I was back—or so I thought.

Throughout the years, I had my bouts with "mini strokes" or what's known as TIAs (transient ischemic attacks). It shocked me to learn that once you have one stroke, you're more likely to have multiple strokes. I'd been to numerous hospitals in Chicago. Doctors couldn't understand why someone so young was experiencing these issues so frequently. In 2009, they diagnosed me with a severe stress disorder; stress was the culprit. I had to learn how to keep my stress levels balanced if I wanted to remain healthy.

However, I didn't know how to decrease my workload. I had a household with seven children, so which one was not supposed to get my best? There were people depending on me, so who was I supposed to say "no" to?

Despite my health issues, I'd powered through to complete my master's degree in 2011. In 2012, after being enrolled for a few weeks in my doctoral program, I experienced a hiccup. When I went to the doctor, he'd given me a look that I knew too well.

"I'm doing too much again, right?" I asked, already knowing his response.

His advice was that I let school go—either that, or potentially have another full-blown stroke. This was heartbreaking for me because going to school was one of the few things that I did for

9

myself. It was my chance to get out of the house and engage in intellectual conversation with people my age. Now, for reasons beyond my control, I had to walk away from something I loved. It was an extremely difficult decision that I agonized over for days. Ultimately, and with great sadness, I opted to withdraw from school.

Maintaining "good" health felt like a punishment. There were so many compromises I had to constantly make with myself that I'd never had to make before. All for the sake of being healthy. Many times, I didn't feel like it was worth it. I felt totally helpless, as though my life was simply allowing me to live it as opposed to me being able to live it on my own terms.

One fateful night in August 2013, I had another stroke. This was the worst yet.

It was a Sunday, and I'd been feeling "off" all day. By this time, I'd had enough experience with strokes to know what was happening, so I laid down and tried to relax. My husband and I were in the bed watching TV, and I reached out to him to call the ambulance, but before I could finish the sentence, I lost consciousness. I could hear him calling my name, but I couldn't respond. Couldn't open my eyes, couldn't move. I heard him scrounging around to find his phone. He called 911. Paramedics arrived on the scene. I could hear them, but I was still unable to respond. I heard them say they couldn't feel my pulse. They opened my eyelids only for them to close back. Then, I heard what no mother wants to hear.

My two youngest daughters (four and seven at the time) came in the room screaming, "What's wrong with Mommy?"

They were crying, and I could hear my husband trying to console them, to no avail.

"Mommy, wake up," they screamed.

As someone who found her own mother dead, this was NOT what I wanted my girls to witness. But what could I do? I couldn't even open my eyes.

The paramedics carried me to the ambulance. As many stroke encounters as I'd had, I'd never had to be put into an ambulance. I lay there, listening to them working to get my pulse.

One of them said, "It's faint, but I got it."

I just remember laying there thinking, "Jesus, please not like this."

However, I was powerless. Lifeless. All I knew was that I didn't want this to be the end of the road for me. My babies needed me.

At some point, we arrived at the hospital. I remember first wiggling my toes. Then, moving my fingers. Finally, opening my eyes. Everything was a blur. I looked around and saw my husband. I could tell that I'd really frightened him. Needless to say, I was in the hospital for a while. Same protocols: MRIs, EKGs, EEGs.

I was fed up, but this time not with the process; I was frustrated with myself. I had to make better decisions. This stroke thing was trying to take me out. It took months before I recovered, but this time was different. This time, I made a conscious choice to do things differently. I was determined to figure out how to do less, how to say no, how to take better care of myself. I still had children to raise, so that didn't change, but for the people outside of my household, I exercised the word "no" more frequently. That seemingly small gesture allowed me to reclaim some time that I could now allocate for resting.

My stroke journey hasn't been easy. It required many behavioral changes. It mandated increasing my awareness about how I treat myself and allow myself to be treated. I had to get control of my stress levels by creating an atmosphere conducive for positive, balanced energy.

It's been ten years since my last stroke. I know it could happen again, but I will not live in fear. Sure, I have some memory loss and struggle from time to time with bouts of aphasia, but that's to be expected. I don't beat myself up over it. I make the most of my good days. I embrace change. I understand that every day may not look

11

the same, and that's okay. I've set boundaries for myself and others as well. I've become an ambassador for strokes, committing myself to educate and empower others about this condition. What I didn't know earlier could have killed me. My life was spared multiple times, and that's something I will always be grateful for and will never forget.

***

Toneal M. Jackson is a national and international award-winning author and filmmaker. She is the founder of Artists Promoting Success, an organization that specializes in helping independent authors and creative artists learn how to succeed as entrepreneurs. More than just a literary talent, Toneal serves as a transformational speaker, coach, and podcaster. Despite the platform, her mission is to educate and empower! For more on Toneal, visit her website: MyNameIsToneal.com.

2 | Another Chance for Life by LaVern Spencer McCarthy

One February evening, I agreed to go to a nightclub with Randy, a man I had known since childhood. Little did I know what fate held in store. I was a single mother of three children, Allen, aged sixteen, Angela, aged fifteen, and Anthony, aged eight. I worked hard to keep them in school and to give them a place to live and something to eat. The older two looked out for the youngest while I worked, and everything was great in our lives at that point.

Randy and my brother were friends and had served together in the Vietnam war. I had dated Randy in the past, but we stopped seeing each other for about six years. He seemed to lose interest in our romance, and I moved on. He showed up at the restaurant where I worked, and our romance was rekindled. I had seen him a couple of weeks before, and he seemed despondent. However, he was cheerful the night we went out on a date as we made our way to a nightclub, The Dance Factory. It was the first time he ever asked me to go to a night club.

As a Vietnam veteran, Randy endured plenty of bad experiences during his service years. He was wounded in action when he stepped on a land mine. Unknown to me, he had also become addicted to street drugs.

We had a pleasant evening at the club. We had a couple of mixed drinks and we danced and talked about many things. He told me about his mother going back to college to become a journalist, and we compared notes on how tedious our jobs were. He then told me about a concert he had recently attended. I suggested we see a concert and he agreed. He gave me a small, red plastic sword that came with the drinks and said, "Keep this to remember me by."

Then he looked at his watch and said it was time to go, as it was getting late. I agreed, and we left. When we got into his double decker pickup truck, he turned on the motor and the radio. He didn't talk much; I assumed he was listening to the radio. I didn't talk either; I was enjoying the moment. I thought he was taking me home, but he began to drive aimlessly around the area for the next twenty minutes.

Suddenly, he had an odd look on his face and turned directly into the path of an oncoming car. I screamed and he returned to the right lane.

Before I realized it, we were in another town, going down a street that crossed railroad tracks. I looked to my right and saw a train rumbling toward us.

He said, "There's the train. Do you think we can beat it?"

It was too close. We could not. I yelled, "No! Stop!"

Instead of hitting the brake, he stepped on the gas.

I immediately opened the door and tumbled out of the car just before impact. The last thing I remembered was going into a soft, velvet darkness as I landed on the asphalt.

When I regained consciousness, several EMTs were around me. I was three feet from the railroad tracks. I smelled my own blood, but I could not see anything because I was blinded by battery acid.

I asked about Randy, and someone said, "He's dead, but you're still alive. We have to get you to the hospital."

I found out later that the train had dragged Randy and his truck down the tracks several hundred yards.

They loaded me into an ambulance that had no springs, and every bump was agony. My mind was numb, but I knew I'd been seriously hurt. I felt thankful when we reached the hospital. My hip and pelvis were broken, and my left arm was crushed. I had a four-inch cut in my head as well as a concussion. I had to have traction on my arm to stop the pain. I wondered if I would ever recover. I was furious this had happened.

14

Meanwhile, my family had been contacted and were frightened that I might not make it. My children stayed with my mother until they could stay at home alone and be safe. The older children were happy to pitch in and do housework while I was healing. It was not a fun time for anyone. Thankfully, the children received survivors' benefits from their deceased father, so we didn't have to worry about money. My husband had died in a car crash years before. I was a widow.

At the hospital, the doctor said, "I can try to repair your left arm with surgery, but if I cannot, I will have to take it off at the elbow."

"I will take that risk," I replied.

I underwent a surgery that took many hours. Afterward he told me, "There was barely enough bone, only about a quarter of an inch to attach a titanium plate that would hold my arm together."

I wore a removable cast for six months and endured countless trips to the doctor's office for X-rays to see if the arm was healing correctly. They would turn it in several directions to get a good picture, and the pain was agonizing. I had to use a cane for almost a year. The physicians also cleaned the battery acid from my eyes, and I could finally see. My left arm ended up being an inch shorter than my right, and I have a four-inch scar from the ordeal. They told me it was a miracle that I lived through this tragedy.

I learned that every bone in Randy's body was broken. It devastated his parents. They visited me at the hospital, and his mother could not stop weeping. She asked, "Did Randy ever talk to you about taking his own life?"

"No," I answered, "but he once said he didn't have anything to live for. It never occurred to me he was serious."

I do not believe they ever knew Randy used drugs. I found out from my brother that the drug, LSD, was Randy's favorite.

I have always thought Randy decided to kill himself, and he did not want to go alone. In those days, there were not many services to help returning veterans of the war. If there had been, Randy's and my life might have been different.

For a long time, I was furious about what had happened and especially angry that my brother didn't tell me Randy was a drug user. I was thirty-two years old and had my life ahead of me. I could not understand how a person I trusted could do such a horrific thing. It was lucky I survived and that my children did not become orphans, having to face the cold world without a mother.

It took over a year for my bones to heal. I ate well, tried to move around as much as possible, took vitamins and tried to keep a positive outlook. I had a loving family who helped and guided me every step of the way. I am deeply thankful to the doctors and nurses who cared for me during my darkest hours.

I was able to see my children grow up and live their own lives.

The incident made me a stronger person. I went to a training college and got a certificate to do office work, a job that paid me well. Later, I became the author of twelve books.

My instincts were sharpened because of the accident, and I have become observant of people. And I taught my kids to be observant of who and what is around them.

Although regaining my health and strength was a challenge, somehow, I have been able to live the wonderful life I have always dreamed of. I am thankful every day for it.

***

LaVern Spencer McCarthy has written and published twelve books of poetry and fiction. Her work has appeared in *Writers and Readers Magazine*; *Meadowlark Reader*; *Agape Review*; *Bards Against Hunger*; *Metastellar*; *Down in the Dirt*; *The Evening Universe*; *Fresh Words Magazine*; *Wicked Shadows Press*; *Midnight Magazine*; *Pulp Cult Press* and others. She is a life member of Poetry Society of Texas. She resides in Blair, Oklahoma where she is currently writing her sixth book of short stories.

3 | Was My Sunday School Teacher Right All Along by Tracey Croisier

It was the second blind date I'd ever agreed to. Ken was a handsome lawyer who volunteered with Habitat for Humanity. We met at an Italian restaurant in New York, down in the village. We ordered appetizers and chatted easily about everything. He'd grown up in a large family of six kids where everyone got along so well that they still vacation together. He said he was hoping to have at least four children.

Wow. It was unusual for a man to talk so openly about marriage and procreation. Any other normal woman on this planet would have counted herself lucky.

But I wasn't a normal woman. I had known for two decades that I could not have children.

I nodded, took a last nosh on the caprese salad, and packed up to leave.

"That sounds lovely. It truly does. Unfortunately, I am not the woman for you. I am barren."

The air felt still, as though I had over shared. He implored me to at least stay and have a good dinner. Maybe we could date a while, maybe there were workarounds, some options.

Pffft. Options! I didn't have a pithy way of explaining that God cursed me at a young age, for reasons entirely unclear and unfair, and that he surely would not want to join defective me in the smiting zone.

When I first started having seizures at age seven, I asked my Sunday school teacher, Mrs. Rex, "Is God mad at me?"

She looked at me kindly and quickly responded, "Oh, no, no, child, God loves you."

Humph. If seizures were his idea of love, then no thank you.

17

At age ten, I was told I could not bear children.

I returned to Mrs. Rex, wanting answers, damnit. Surely God had jinxed me. How else could you explain being pronounced infertile before I even had my first period? Also, what about that gross boy that picks his nose and punches everyone during church, right in front of God? What's his punishment for being an intentionally crappy kid?

In her pristine, knobby knit pencil skirt, Mrs. Rex kneeled down, so we were eye to eye, "It is all part of God's plan for you," she replied, confident that this was the best answer to give a hurting tween.

It haunted me for decades after, the way she smiled and gave my elbow a squeeze, beaming, as if to imply that I had, indeed, won an awesome prize.

Naturally, I stayed furious at God—and his PR gal, Mrs. Rex—for eons.

As though a child-free life was my choice, I leaned in to all that lifestyle offered. I worked long, hard hours on Wall Street. I splurged on a weekly cleaner and pricey leather goods. I was lucky to marry a lovely man who did not want children.

This felt like quite the coup. Take that, Mrs. Rex! Someone loves me because of my inability to procreate. In moments of doubt, I would wonder if the lovely man was part of God's plan? Maybe Mrs. Rex was half-right.

I stored whatever sadness about my lot in life in a slim-necked carafe in my left rib cage, an inch from my heart. The grey, lumpy sadness stayed contained, except on New Year's Eve.

For ten years, the lovely man and I would trek south to Darien, CT, to celebrate with our closest friends, sisters Fran and Suzi and their families. They each had two children, and I was known for my ability to get any baby to fall asleep. It wasn't that hard: I explained economic factors and how they affected interest rates, and, voila! A sleeping baby.

Sometime after midnight, everyone loose and blurry, Suzi would thank me for taking the kids off her hands for a bit.

"You would be such a good mother," she'd say, slowly and deliberately. "Fran and I were just talking about it yesterday; you just really have fun with children."

I'd remind her of my defective reproductive bits. Then, either Suzi's warm embrace or the champagne and the sad carafe cork would pop off and I'd openly weep big, fat, angry, hot, phlegmy tears.

"I know, I know," Suzi would coo. "Just don't give up, though. That's all. There are ways, you know."

Part of our New Year's Eve ritual was that I would then sob the entire drive home. We'd sit in our driveway, waiting for me to funnel the barfy sadness back into its container. The lovely man would have something amazingly pithy and profound to say, and we'd return to our double income, no kids (DINK) life as though nothing odd had transpired.

Then September 11th happened, and the lovely man and I grieved differently. We divorced, and I moved west to Seattle. The universe gave me a second chance at love, and I married a second time.

Armed with Suzi's "don't give up" mantra rolled into a little pearlescent soft ball, next to the sadness bottle, my new husband James and I decided to try in vitro fertilization. Insurance did not cover IVF, so we could afford just one cycle. We were told donor eggs would have the highest success rate.

Egg-shopping is a dauntingly odd odyssey. For six months I scoured online egg donation websites. Oh, how I wanted the egg donor to look like me, lest a passerby notice that I didn't match my baby. Worse yet, I was terrified that my offspring would love me less when they realized I didn't match them.

I found a doppelgänger in the Midwest and eagerly awaited her medical history and detailed bio, hoping for a fellow book nerd, a crossword fan, maybe a lap swimmer. I was gobsmacked to learn she was not a librarian, but a tattooed pole dancer. She waxed eloquently about Dolly Parton's physique. She was hoping the egg donation money would help her afford breast augmentation surgery.

Nature vs. nurture smacked us upside the head. James and I felt it was important that we have an open relationship with the egg donor. That is, we wanted to meet the donor in person, and we wanted a donor that would be willing to sustain a relationship with us and our children. We struggled with tying our fate to someone so very different than us. I'll admit to heaving a sigh of relief when the dancer said she would never consider an open relationship.

My epic quest for a look-alike egg donor came to a screeching halt when James casually suggested I search for a creative egg donor. "It would be horrible if you gave birth to a serious engineer, even if they looked exactly like you."

In an instant, I showed him Lena's profile. I bookmarked Lena in my very first week of egg searching and when I saw her picture; I swear it glowed; it sparkled. She was physically my polar opposite: lean with dark brown hair past her shoulders, glacier blue eyes.

Lena was a photographer and jewelry designer, and her relatives were equally creative.

I yearned for her and her genetics in a way that defied logic. The egg broker recommended I compose an essay, maybe a couple of paragraphs, to give Lena an idea of what we were like. My 'small essay' stretched over six pages. I started with the painful truth:

"I'd like to think that I've spent more time than anyone yearning to have children. Some people may try to get pregnant for a decade, but I've been wanting a child of my own since 1974." I walked Lena through the ridiculousness of being barren at age ten, at the shocking surprise pregnancy (despite three forms of birth control) that set my world on fire, the kind first husband, the wedding photo of me and James in Hawaii. I threw in dog and cat photos and, for good measure, a recipe for a dairy free smoothie. My heart laid bare.

To our astonishment, she said yes. She would happily donate her eggs in our quest for children. And, yes, she would be willing to have an open relationship.

Astoundingly, all three of us had fallen in love with our collective vision for our future.

It worked! We installed two embryos in February and eight months later; I gave birth to twin girls at the tender young age of forty-four.

Surprisingly, birthing my twins smashed my bottle of sadness into a million jagged shards. For the first six months postpartum, I could not stop weeping, both with joy because Suzi was right; I am a good and fun mom. But also because my brain needed to mourn all those long years that I was mad, shaking my fist at the universe and God, furious that everyone else got to be happy except me. Irate that Mrs. Rex seemed so dang confident that she knew this invisible, incommunicado God had a plan for me.

Do my twins look like me? Maybe. They each have my winning smile and sense of humor.

When they look at me, they see mom, the woman who fed them roasted figs with blue cheese, who took them to swimming lessons at the YMCA, because that's what my mom did. I am also the mom who told them their amazing three-person birth story every night for years, to pay homage to honesty and good fortune.

When I gaze at their lovely faces, I am reminded of the immense, insane kindness of strangers and that, yes, everyone gets second chances, so long as you are brave enough to dream up and execute your plan.

And I think that maybe, just maybe, Mrs. Rex was right: God did have one heck of an awesome plan for me.

***

Tracey Croisier lives with her family in the Seattle area and works as a high school librarian. She's active in the storytelling community and has won six Moth StorySLAMs. When not shelving books or carpooling with her daughters, Tracey enjoys hot yoga and outrigger canoeing on Lake Washington. She's currently working on *You Done Us Wrong*, an historical novel about Carrie Buck and the still-legal practice of sterilizing "unfit" women in the United States.

4 | Racing Ahead by Andrew Shelffo

I'm lined up with thousands of other runners, waiting for this St. Patrick's Day 10k race to start, and it hits me: I'm going to die.

Six weeks ago, I was in the hospital, in intensive care after a heart attack. Earlier that day, I felt like I had food stuck in my throat. I went to the local Urgent Care so that someone could take it out. While I was there, the provider, a brusque woman in her forties with her hair pulled back in a ponytail, insisted that I have an EKG, which didn't seem necessary.

She left the room and then a technician came in, pushing a portable EKG machine. She stuck sensors on my chest, hit a button, and then tore off the printout the machine spat out. She then took the sensors off—along with a lot of chest hair—smiled at me and walked out of the room.

A few minutes later, the provider came back into the room, holding the printout. She handed it to me and said, "You need to get to the hospital immediately. I've called an ambulance."

Deep down, I'm a rule follower, so I did what the provider asked. She seemed sufficiently—but professionally—concerned. So I knew I couldn't ignore this medical advice, even though all I could think about was what a hassle this was turning out to be. I was in the ICU just a few hours later, the one-hundred percent blocked artery now clear. I was also the proud owner of a brand-new stent.

This was all a complete surprise; it came totally out of the blue. And through it all, I just kept thinking that my heart attack didn't happen like it did in the movies. I didn't clutch my chest. I didn't experience a lot of pain. I didn't even think I belonged in the hospital.

The truth is, I got screwed. For my entire life, I've followed the rules. I've eaten right, seen the doctor regularly, and exercised. I average more than one salad per day, for crying out loud. I asked the cardiologist why this happened to me, someone who has no risk factors.

He shrugged. "Sometimes it just happens."

That made me mad, but mad at who?

And just like that, I'm now a heart-attack survivor.

In the hospital, they put me into a protocol, just like every other heart patient. Here are the drugs you're going to take for the rest of your life. Here are the stats on heart attacks patients that I'm going to quote to you when you ask questions. Here's the diet we now want you to follow.

But I'm different. I know I'm different, because I feel different. I'm young. Or at least, at fifty-six, on the younger side of the stats. I don't have a family history of heart attacks. I don't smoke.

But I also know I am just like everyone else. We're all going to die.

People look at me differently now.

A colleague at work asked me the other day at lunch, "How are you doing?" which differs from just asking, "How are you?"

This question demands a more thorough response. But I know what's happening. This colleague is roughly my age. He's expressing concern, sure, but he's also looking for differences between me and him, something—anything—so he can believe that what happened to me won't happen to him. As I tell him the details of my health saga, I can see that he's not reassured. And I imagine that his thinking shifts to thinking I'm damaged goods. Fragile and weak. Anything to differentiate himself from me.

A few weeks after I got out of the hospital, I started cardiac rehab, a program recommended by the cardiologist. There, I exercised under the close supervision of nurses and while wearing a heart monitor. I was the youngest person there by decades. And I was the only one who would bring workout clothes. Most everyone else worked out in jeans.

One day, I heard one of the older guys say to the nurse, "I'm only doing this so I can get to twelve sessions and get out of here!"

It surprised me to hear him say that, because when I looked at him, I saw someone who clearly needed rehab. In contrast, I knew I didn't belong there. But the guidelines are the guidelines.

I did the twelve sessions, and I finished the program. On my last day, I got a certificate, a T-shirt, and I rang a bell. I also got medical clearance to run again.

And today, I'm getting ready to run a race.

The starting cannon goes off, and we all surge forward.

All I wanted, in the hospital, in the ICU, in rehab, was for someone to say that I was different, that my recovery would be easier because I'd done such a decent job of following the rules. No one said that. Not the cardiologist, not the attending physician, not the nurses in ICU, and not the nurses in cardiac rehab. Every single one of them would smile professionally at me and remind me of the new rules to follow.

"Not too much sodium. Avoid red meat. Watch the stress. Wear sunblock."

On my last day of rehab, I triumphantly told the nurse, "I'm going to run in this race."

She responded, "That reminds me: be sure to look out for bleeding problems."

Bleeding problems? Seriously?

And now I'm working hard to get up this first big hill in the race. I can feel the small glass vial of nitroglycerin tablets in my pocket. I'm supposed to take them if I have chest pains, and I'm supposed to keep them with me wherever I go.

I'm pushing it now. My heart is pounding. This is the hardest it's worked since before the heart attack. I've run this race many times. I've run a lot of races, and I know how easily worry can take over. I could trip over an untied shoelace. I could step in a pothole and twist an ankle. I could shit myself.

25

Now I have a new worry, that my heart is going to explode.

Okay, I have learned enough about cardiac anatomy to know that a heart can't actually explode. But I can still picture myself collapsing at some point in the race.

I'm at mile two now. The next big hill awaits at mile three.

From the moment I went to urgent care, through the trip to the ICU and the stent procedure, and in the hospital and later in rehab, I never thought I'd die. But now I'm thinking about precisely that. But there are ambulances here and medical personnel. I console myself with the thought that the chances of dying are slim.

The hill at mile three is the biggest one. It's where I benefit most from the neighbors who are standing in front of their houses cheering and offering bottles of water. Their energy gives me a boost.

How am I doing? Not good. My breathing sounds like a freight train. I'm sweating like it's one-hundred degrees outside, and I'm seriously wondering if I will be able to finish this race.

"You don't look so good," a spectator says to me.

He's right, but I still feel insulted. I look up at him, because I've been looking down at my feet as I climbed the last hill, and he's smiling. Now I'm confused.

Then I see what he has in his hand: a can of beer. "You look like you could use one of these."

I'll never fully heal from this heart attack. The fact is, I now have a twenty-five percent chance of having another heart attack within two years. Also, my life expectancy has declined by about ten percent. I'm not afraid of dying, but I am mad about all the things I might miss if I do.

Like I said, I may be different, but I'm also just like everyone else: we're all going to die.

I take the beer from his hand and keep on running.

***

Andrew Shelffo is a writer, teacher, and storyteller who lives in western Massachusetts. He spent his formative years in New Jersey and still waxes poetic about New Jersey's food and the unique driving habits of its residents.

5 | Life with Father by John Hahm

Growing up in Hawaii with my Korean American father and Japanese American mother, I sometimes felt as though I were living in the shadow of an active volcano. Between the terrible eruptions of that volcano, my childhood was quite happy. My younger siblings, my childhood friends, and I grew up reveling in all the goofy joys that all children know. I clearly remember my father's happy smile as he tossed us high into the air and caught us at the last second. But every so often, that volcano—my all-powerful Aba-ji, my father—would blow its top. My father would come home angry, and that anger would be fueled by some white-hot force that only my mother—my Okaasan—understood. And she would talk to him and calm him down.

"Why was Aba-ji so mad?" I'd ask her the next day, as we waited on the porch for a yellow school bus to take me to the Baptist kindergarten. "And what's a curse? He said there was a curse on him."

Okaasan would reply, "There's no such thing as a curse. Aba-ji just says that when mean things happen to him, that he doesn't understand. I think the War hurt him and sometimes made him angry. But never mind. Here's your bus! Have fun at kindergarten!"

My father wasn't always angry. He was the smart, gentle giant who helped us with our science fair projects and tutored us in algebra.

My father's outbursts didn't happen often. But they were unpredictable, and they were unforgettable. Mom thought the War had filled my dad with his deep-seated hurt and anger. No doubt it did, at least in part. Aba-ji had been an Army staff-sergeant, a twice-wounded combat-infantryman. He'd fought in Guadalcanal and the Philippines, two of the bloodiest campaigns against the Japanese.

28

We saw that he carried haunting memories of those battles. And we intuited that there were other old wounds, too. So Aba-ji would sometimes explode and burst our childhood joys, and send us running for cover.

But that wouldn't happen today! I was a high school junior now, with my share of success stories under my skinny belt. And today would be the happiest day of my seventeen years of life. Today at the dinner table I would tell my all-powerful Aba-ji something that had to make him happy. It was guaranteed!

"Pop, I've been accepted at Northwestern University. I'm going to major in English there."

"English! Don't be stupid!" he said. "You're not going to waste a Northwestern education on English! What kind of engineer do you want to be?"

I couldn't bear to hear him put down my cherished dreams of studying and teaching English.

"If you're an engineer," he said, "you'll never have to live hand-to-mouth. Look at the Yoshizaki boy up the street. Only twenty-six, and he has a house and a car already. And engineers have clout in this world. They make the machines that move mountains and build our world."

I said, "And writers and teachers shaped the imaginations of those engineers and helped us all make a better world."

I reminded him that he'd promised me I could choose my own field of study and create my own destiny once I got to college. Damn! Aba-ji had managed to turn my biggest triumph into my most bitterly frustrated desire to date.

Just his unsmiling face would have been enough to unnerve me. At last, he shouted, "Pabo!"

I heard equal parts anger and heartbreak in his voice.

He shouted it again, louder, this time in pure anger, "Pabo!"

Pabo means fool in Korean. But the way he said it, it meant "Traitor!" I had betrayed my father's long cherished dream, that his

29

eldest son would achieve the profession he had so desired in life but had been denied. As the second youngest of ten children in his family, my father got no support for any college education. And there was one more cruel frustration propelling my father's ire. His father had disowned him when he fell in love with my Japanese American mother and married her over his father's vitriolic condemnations and threats. Aba-ji thought it would redeem him in his father's eyes if I fulfilled his frustrated ambitions by achieving an engineering degree.

"You're not going to Northwestern. If you want that shitty degree in English, the University of Hawaii is good enough for you. And you're paying your own way. Work in the pineapple cannery if you want to go to college. Damn you, John!" my father concluded. "There's a curse on this family, and you're a curse on me!"

There it was. The notion of an inexorable, unbeatable cosmic force in the universe that frustrated a good man's deepest aspirations. But as I saw it, now my own father was doing to me what his father had done to him. There were no occult cosmic forces here. There were only fathers projecting onto their sons the cruelest frustrations of their own lives. Korean men pride themselves on being stubborn. Well, I'm Korean too, I told myself. And I girded myself for a long struggle of wills with my father. This would be the last time I let him, or anyone else, foreclose on my future.

In my senior year in high school, I worked the night shift at Dole Pineapple Cannery. That summer, I worked double-shifts there hoping to fund not just my studies at the University of Hawaii, but some part of my hoped-for course work at Northwestern University. I took the bus to the cannery on Lewers Street and enlisted in the Pineapple Core. I rushed to beat the shrill steam whistle that started my work shifts.

The cannery comprised a series of dangerous machines, forming a kind of mechanical snake. The whole cannery thrummed and hissed and clattered with a kind of samba rhythm. It was a symphony of mechanical, steam, and electrical sounds that almost made you forget how easy it would be to get lacerated, scalded, or shocked by machines that didn't know you from a pineapple.

I cycled through several jobs at the cannery, each paying a little more than the last. The best paying job was also the most dangerous. This was the slicer-machine cleanup detail. I had to clean out the slicer blade assemblies on the machines that turned slugs of peeled, cored pineapple into uniform slices of fruit, ready for canning. I still shudder at the memory of those thirty-inch, claw-shaped, giant razor blades. You had to make sure the blades were balanced right, because those rows of blades might swing down under their own weight. There was a slotted metal cylinder in the center of the machine, through which the slicer blades slashed with a ker-chunking sound. Then we washed and cleaned each of those giant razor blades, which were only a half-inch apart. There were always some stubborn shreds of pineapple stuck on the blades. We had to peel these off with our bare hands and wash down any sticky spots.

I did well at this job and got several pay raises doing it. Then I got careless. All of us "veterans" let down our guard around those slicer blades. Early one morning, a guy about my age lost his arm cleaning the slicer machine. I quit the job the next night. How long would I survive in that place of raw electricity and sharp-edged steel? Would I always make the right moves, in the right sequence, and never make a mistake? I was terrified to think of the mistakes I would certainly make when I was tired. And it was time I stopped thinking of myself as being in an all-out war of wills with my father. That kind of thinking had led me to this terrible choice of a higher paying but deadly industrial job.

I was awarded a scholarship from the Korean American Students' Association at the University of Hawaii. I didn't have to work at dangerous jobs to spite my father. From now on, I would work intelligently to achieve my goals. I was no longer trying to best my father in a battle of wills. And in my senior year at UH, I was accepted to the Graduate School of Northwestern University, where I would study English!

But once again, I felt the heavy hand of my father pressing down on my shoulder. He opposed my going to Northwestern for graduate work in English and refused to contribute financially. But this time, I was ready for him. I'd secretly joined this prestigious travel club called the U.S. Navy. Northwestern agreed to postpone my formal matriculation date, and I would go there on the GI Bill. My father was flabbergasted that I'd done this. He had to admit that I was tenacious, moving mountains to study literature and writing at Northwestern. But I assured him I hadn't done this to prove myself more stubborn than he. I had merely taken responsibility for my own future.

I made my peace with my father. I remember how proud and happy he looked when I came home in my dress white uniform with the Lieutenant jg's shoulder boards. This was at the end of my long stint in the U.S. Navy. He took me to his workplace at Shop Fifty-One, the electrical shop at the submarine base in Pearl Harbor Naval Shipyard, to show me off to his workmates and to the Navy commanders in charge. I felt as happy that day as he did. We were no longer a father and son at war.

A few years later, as a successful high school English teacher in Chicago, I took my wife and two small children to meet their grandparents. They treated us to an authentic Hawaiian feast, a luau, which lasted late into the night.

As my wife and I packed our over-tired little boy and grumpy little girl for the drive back to our hotel, I heard my dad telling my aunts and uncles. "You know, all my other kids never talk back to me. Only John. He was the only one who did. He always had to do things the hard way! Stubborn, that one!"

And I heard his brother laugh and answer, "He's just like you then!"

My dad was quiet for a while. And then he said, "Yeah. He's just like me."

***

John Hahm is a Chicago writer, storyteller, and an aspiring tanguero (tango dancer). He grew up in Honolulu, Hawaii, and got his MA in English at Northwestern University after a stint in the U.S. Navy. He recently retired from teaching at Northside College Prep High School, where he taught AP English, British, American and World Literature, Creative Writing, and coached the Academic Decathlon Team. He continues to learn from some of the best writers and storytellers in Chicago, who are his friends.

6 | Between Worlds: A Journey of Near-Death Insights by Liza Anderson

They delivered last rites. I was dying on the ventilator.

It all began the night before my fifty-second birthday. In two days, I went from having stomach pains to eventually being admitted to the Surgical ICU. I could no longer breathe on my own. My husband, John, signed a consent form to put me on life support and place me in an induced coma.

John told me later everything that happened while I was fighting for my life in the coma.

My two stepdaughters, Lisa and Aubrey, arrived with flowers and balloons to visit. They had no idea what had transpired. They were unprepared to see my hands restrained to the bed, connected to both breathing and feeding tubes. Their surprise turned to worry when they saw their usually stoic father break down in tears.

It all began with my visit to the doctor for severe stomach pains. My doctor thought the pain might be due to complications from an appendix surgery I had fourteen years earlier, so he sent me to the ER for more tests. The ER doctors ordered an ultrasound, ignored the notes from my doctor, and kept me over the weekend, treating me for dehydration and pain. Physicians said the ultrasound was inconclusive and ordered a CT scan for two days later. It felt too long to wait, but we were at their mercy. It was 10 p.m. on a Friday.

On the morning of the CT scan, a nurse told me to drink two liters of barium even though I couldn't drink or eat for three days. As they rolled me on the gurney, I felt nauseous. I vomited right in the CT scanner. When I came out of the scanner, I felt I'd blown up to twice my size. Eight doctors surrounded me. One said I looked blue, and the nurse who gave me the barium was crying. They rushed me to critical care, which is when John arrived.

I learned later that I continued to get weaker. The X-rays showed I developed Acute Respiratory Distress Syndrome (ARDS), which is worse than pneumonia; oxygen can't get into the body. So now I battled two life-threatening issues simultaneously. A resident doctor told my husband the only hope was to put me in an induced coma and move me to the Surgical ICU.

John remembered a critical care doctor taking him aside and saying, "Your wife is critically ill and may not make it," as he touched my husband's shoulder.

That night, my husband began planning my funeral.

As John headed home around midnight, he went to a church that remained open around the clock to pray that I would somehow come out of this. We had a vacation scheduled to celebrate our anniversary in July, and John later told me he thought he would still go alone and try to find me there. He expected me to pass away.

The next day, Aubrey, Lisa, and my husband stayed with me, holding guard-style shifts, as they felt I needed an advocate. During this time, I developed a blood clot, another cause for concern. They no longer trusted in the care that I was receiving, even though I was at a major academic medical center in the heart of downtown Chicago.

While my friends and family prayed for me during my three weeks in a coma, I had two profound experiences. But time did not run linearly like on Earth because all my experiences happened simultaneously.

In one journey, I found myself in a hotel room instructed to watch the movie of my life. I understood that after watching I'd be going to heaven. I didn't see what was on the television screen, but I felt a warm, comforting feeling while the movie played. I felt complete peace and love. At the end of the movie, I realized I was still alive and wondered why. I walked out of the room to the end of a dark hallway. There was an entity there, but it was not Jesus or God.

35

The entity pointed to the left and said, "If you choose this way, you will drift off and can be so happy." Then he pointed to the right. "But if you choose this way, you will suffer much, but eventually, you will be okay."

I was very drawn to just slipping away. I knew it would be so easy.

I asked, "But if I go left, wouldn't that be like committing suicide?"

The entity immediately disappeared, and I knew I would not die. Apparently, because I was uncertain, the entity took that as my answer. But in my heart, I held the unwavering conviction that both paths were open to me, and God would have allowed whichever one I chose. It would all be okay, no matter what happened. There was not a wrong choice.

I found this a little confusing because the bible says that God knows the exact time of death and that He has appointed it. If this is the case, why did I feel I had a choice? At that moment, I realized there was so much we don't know about death.

I clearly wasn't ready to go. I had so much life left to live with John, and so many things we planned to do and see together. I didn't want to leave him. I wanted to live the life I'd planned: trips, moving to a new location, and eventually retirement. I thought of how John had a difficult early adulthood due to a divorce from his first wife, and he didn't deserve to have me die so young.

I took another journey where I found myself underwater in an ocean. Shadows, and what looked like people floated by me, but no one I knew. I moved around freely, then suddenly, I was shot up through the water.

I was face-to-face with a brilliant light and a figure in bright white robes. I thought it was Jesus, although some people might call it Buddha, God, Mohammed, etc. I felt it in my heart and every part of my being. Initially, standing there, I could not look directly at Him because He was too bright.

He asked me to look at Him and said, "Don't worry about everything swirling around you; just look at Me. Focus on Me."

And when I did, I felt complete unconditional love, no judgment whatsoever, only beauty. I felt at peace and that everything would be okay no matter what happened to me.

When I looked into His eyes, it was ethereal. In all my life, I had never seen anything close to the beauty of Jesus' eyes. His eyes were a kaleidoscope of many different colors that reflected infinity. Then, after looking into His eyes, Jesus touched my left shoulder, and I spiraled downward. At this point, I felt I woke up and came out of the coma.

For the next three weeks, I remained in the hospital with a breathing tube and IVs in place.

I could not eat or swallow food. After four major surgeries, I spent the entire month of June in rehab. As I slowly reclaimed my body, I now had the yeoman's job of getting healthy again. I needed to learn to breathe, swallow, talk, and walk without assistance.

But I felt differently about my recovery as a result of my experiences. I never felt like a victim or placed blame on anyone. I somehow felt that Jesus was present with me through it at each step. I am sure my body started to heal because I did not resist what was happening to me. I strongly felt that whatever was going to happen was in His hands, and it would be okay no matter what happened.

In those initial months, tears became a regular companion. I encountered so many scary moments.

Like the time one of the doctors told John, "If your wife does not start breathing on her own by tomorrow, we will have to give her a tracheotomy."

As I overheard this, tears started streaming down my eyes. Would this be my new normal? The prospect of never breathing on my own again weighed heavily on my heart.

John held my trembling hands and said, "Liza, I know you can do this."

He then told the doctors, "We have to give it a little more time. We don't want a tracheotomy."

Amidst my tears, a sense of calmness washed over me. It was as if I could feel Jesus by my side. A deep realization settled in— the assurance that I was loved and looked after. I trusted that I was being supported and that no matter how things unfolded, it would be okay. And so, as the sun rose on the following day, I breathed independently.

"I knew you could do it," said one of my favorite doctors, giving me a high five.

Tears of joy streamed down my face as John and I held each other close. This win was a turning point for me in my recovery.

Each time I faced a challenge like that, even though it seemed insurmountable, I knew I could bear it.

"Jesus," I cried out. "Please be with me during this suffering. Sit with me through it." And I felt He was there. During the long, lonely nights in the hospital. When my hands had to be tied to the bed because there were so many tubes in me, I would pull them out without knowing it. For the daily medical tests and X-rays because the doctors still had to rule out cancer. When I had to care for and monitor the unsettling scars healing from my four surgeries. The warmth of that love and support I received from Him made these moments the happiest I've ever been. Amazingly, something so horrific was also the best gift I had ever received.

When I reflect back on the months of brutal physical therapy, excruciating pain, and numerous setbacks, I believed that the message I got when I almost died was that things will constantly be swirling around me in this life. But, if I can just keep my focus on Him ("Just look at Me"), He will guide me toward the right path. I understood He will get me through even the most horrific events and be there for the joyful times as well.

I have recovered from that challenging experience and lead an active life. I still have some lingering health issues that can affect me, but nothing that keeps me down. And for that, I am grateful. Interestingly, when I was in the coma, I saw my future; my husband and I lived close to the lake with beautiful parks and beaches nearby. Three months after leaving the hospital, my husband and I moved out of the city and close to the lake. I see so many areas around us that I once saw in my coma.

As a result of my experiences, I no longer fear death for myself or my loved ones. I know the journey from this world will be peaceful. I will be given everything I need to transition. It will be just like floating effortlessly into another realm, engulfed in ethereal beauty. It was both exciting and easy. There is no end, just more adventure of the utmost kind.

***

Liza Anderson is a new author. But she is no stranger to storytelling. As a marketing executive in start-ups and not-for-profit organizations, she used storytelling to build brands for over twenty-five years. She recently left the corporate world and is spending time writing a memoir on her near-death experience. In her free time, Liza loves to travel, hike, bike, and spend time in her garden. She finds solace and creativity in nature. She lives in Illinois with her husband and dog.

7 | I Am Not Your Filipina Domestic by Faith R. Kares

I walked back into the coffee shop where I had been working on my laptop, phone in hand, still stunned, and reeling from the unexpected conversation with my dissertation advisor.

"I know your mom was a domestic worker in Hong Kong. So, I hope this isn't too awkward," she said to me over the phone.

Absolutely nothing awkward at all about a white tenured university faculty member asking me—her grad student and the daughter of a Filipina immigrant—to clean her bathroom. For free.

What. The. Fuck.

Let me back up a bit. I was wrapping up my doctorate at Northwestern University, in my fifth year, and writing my dissertation. I was so close to being done. I was scared that my advisor would not sign off on my dissertation if I said no.

So, I did what any self-respecting thirty-something-year-old enmeshed in the feudal system of academia would do: I obliged.

"Uh, sure, when do you need me to come by?" I said quietly, stunned by her request, but knowing it required a prompt reply.

"The sooner the better. I really just need the bathroom done, and the floors, and if you can wipe down the windows and the sink. Oh, and the toilet, of course. If you have time, maybe vacuum the living room."

I later realized that I conceded to her demands because I was so close to completing my Ph.D. I had already put up with her racist behavior and remarks for nearly six years. What was another remark? She was constantly infantilizing me and the other students with whom she worked.

Once when I had to reschedule a meeting with her, she responded over email, "I figured you over-scheduled yourself, you little Faith, you."

She was also protective of my time, insistent that I limit the time I spend as a Teaching Assistant even though I loved it, and teaching was precisely why I pursued a doctorate.

She once emailed, "Absolutely refuse to do anything for that class outside those hours. Good girl, love mom."

Doctoral students often rely on a single individual, their advisor, to succeed. So I trained myself to shrug it off, thinking it would be possible to avoid internalizing these microaggressions.

I remember my partner's response when I shared my advisor's unbelievable request to clean. "Whaaaaaat? Are you serious? Babe, you need to tell HR!"

I replied flatly. "Babe, grad students don't have an HR."

The reality of the culture of Ph.D. programs coupled with my background and upbringing primed me for abuse and exploitation. I grew up in a working-poor, single-parent, immigrant household. I was accustomed to scarcity. I was deeply familiar with the government-issued rectangular blocks of orange cheese, the massive white and silver tubs of peanut butter, and the pitying and judgmental looks of the grocery store cashier when my mom purchased items with food stamps. My mom "shopped" for her three kids at the local soup kitchen, searching through donation boxes, which meant I frequently wore the hand-me-downs of my classmates. I remember holding my breath, hoping that no one would notice their Umbro shorts or Adidas castoffs on me, or that I was likely wearing their jacket from last season, which their parents had donated to the Salvation Army. I ran girls' cross-country, and my first pair of sneakers was my coach's used purple and magenta Asics. But my mom had instilled in me the American Dream—that education would guarantee my socioeconomic success—so I would do whatever it took to obtain my Ph.D. And my advisor knew this.

She frequently reminded me that she made my writing good; she was the reason why I got all the grants and why my research was compelling. By my fifth year in the Ph.D. program, I felt grateful she was hard on me because I thought she was making me better. It was all tough love, right? Thank goodness a nice liberal white lady, like herself, was looking out for little old me, the daughter of a Filipina immigrant.

It was for all of these reasons that I felt I owed her when she posed the egregious request that I clean for her.

"I've always been there for you."

"I've cooked for you hundreds of times."

Indeed, she had cooked for me and many of her other advisees—she always insisted students come to her home for meetings, which frequently took place around dinner time. And now she injured her shoulder and needed help. Who was I to say no?

So, that following Sunday, I scrubbed her bathroom floor on my hands and knees, as she instructed. "That's the best way to clean my floors."

As I scrubbed the floor, I could feel her eyes on me, making sure I performed my unpaid duties with fidelity. "Remember the mirrors."

I wiped down her bathroom mirrors, cleaned the shower, and scrubbed the toilet bowl.

"Oh, and could you also vacuum the living room?"

"Uh, sure."

While cleaning, I wondered why she didn't just hire and pay someone to perform this labor. How could a Marxist, antiracist, feminist treat her grad students like this? Ironically, she taught courses calling attention to the power dynamics undergirding the second-wave women's movement—that the success and workforce advancement of white women was and continues to be heavily subsidized by the bodies of Black and Brown women.

I felt so raw and angry. It felt dehumanizing to be on the floor while this woman watched me clean. My face felt hot, and tears stung the corners of my eyes. I brushed them off with my arm, determined not to cry in front of her. But I felt nauseous, and my chest was tight. I mused to myself that she doesn't need to pay for domestic help because her grad students provide free labor. She already knew I would do whatever it took to succeed because of my background.

After the cleaning, I resolved it would be just this one time. She needed help. And, after all, she had done so much for me. But within twenty-four hours she emailed, requesting I return the following week to continue to "help" her.

I pulled deep from my well of courage, drew a boundary, and responded. "No, I would not have the time to continue to help you."

Immediately, she canceled all our future meetings. And for the next few months, she withdrew support from me but continued advising her other students. These were the students who agreed to "help" her. They cooked for her, did her laundry, and even drove her to hair appointments. All of these "helpers" were women grad students. All unpaid labor.

It was during the Thanksgiving holiday, when I was home in Massachusetts, that I first told my mom the entire story. It had been months, and my advisor was still not speaking to me. She was unresponsive to my emails where I solicited feedback on articles, dissertation chapters, and conference papers. I really needed that feedback. I was going on the academic job market. I was on the brink of my dream to become a university professor. And all that stood between me and that dream was this racist, entitled white lady. I was so naïve to once believe that higher education was the harbinger of equity, when in fact some professors exploit their graduate students so shamelessly.

After I unloaded my story to my mom, she didn't respond right away. She didn't even seem surprised, and mused aloud, "It is amazing I sacrificed so much to come here, for you and your brothers to have a better life, and you get the biggest degree, and still, you clean floors."

I said nothing because I didn't know what to say. I felt sad and frankly ashamed that I hadn't stood up for myself.

The matter-of-factness of my mom's statement woke me up. I was incensed that this type of institution had allowed this level of exploitation. What more of myself would I give up to obtain my degree?

Growing up, I thought if I got the biggest, baddest degree, then maybe people wouldn't talk to me like they did to my mom. They would respect me; they would invite me to sit at their table, instead of asking me to clean it. I naively bought into the American dream, the myth of meritocracy, and believed that with education I could transcend not only poverty but racism.

Sitting at the airport in Boston, waiting for my flight back to Chicago, I knew what I had to do: I needed to change advisors. It's exceedingly rare to do so late in one's doctoral program. But it was no longer worth it to sacrifice my pride and my integrity to be this woman's domestic helper, just to get my Ph.D. I would obtain my degree on my own terms, with my self-esteem intact, and certainly not on my knees, scrubbing someone else's floor.

I changed advisors, working instead with an incredible woman of color who did not require that I scrub her floors to receive constructive feedback on my written work. I shored up the support of the rest of my dissertation committee as well as the Dean of the Graduate School, who strongly denounced my advisor's behavior. In 2015, I graduated with a Ph.D. in Cultural Anthropology at Northwestern University. Since then, I have used my academic training to advance racial justice and gender equity in various spaces including STEM fields and within the Chicago police. More recently, I built the research arm of a pro-Black, pro-Queer, pro-Woman Diversity, Equity, and Inclusion (DEI) nonprofit consulting firm. That voice inside that used to say I owed my success to someone other than myself, to some white lady, is gone. My degree is mine alone. And no one can take that away from me.

***

Dr. Faith R. Kares (she/her) is a writer, researcher, and passionate educator. She is a lover, a dreamer, a friend, an introvert on some days, and an extrovert on others. She is a dog lover, tree hugger, and the proud daughter of a Filipina immigrant woman.

8 | Personal Court of Opinion by Anne Wagner

I didn't sleep.

I thrashed. I was anxious.

My body was vibrating with fear.

It seemed impossible that I would lose my children. Even so, I was on the verge of a panic attack the entire night before court. M., my ex-husband, was mad. Mad that I had left him, mad that I wouldn't move to the north shore suburbs of Chicago to raise our kids, mad that my dad was paying for the special school for our daughter. Mad at himself. And now he was asking a judge to take our daughters to remedy his madness.

"Anne, just get your parents to buy you a house in Wilmette. Come on," he snapped.

We had been divorced for three years. Our oldest daughter had a lot of learning disabilities and I needed to find a new school for her third-grade year. The one I found was expensive, and my dad had generously agreed to pay for it.

"They have better services for free on the North Shore," he pushed.

M. has small black eyes and an unusual way of dressing. He frequently looked like a Jersey Shore refugee mixed with middle-aged suburban style, like he might have a personality disorder or mental disability. Both things may have been true, but what was truer was that he was mean.

I didn't want to live on the North Shore. I had felt like an outsider for most of my life, but that had become worse since becoming a single mom. A sensitivity to whispers about my parenting, career, and children's perceived lack had become a constant in my mind's heart. If I forgot to brush my child's hair for a school event, I knew we would be the subject of gossip. Plus, I liked raising my kids in a city. We were all perfectly misplaced but placed together. More to the point, my parents would never buy me a house in Wilmette, whether they could afford to. Matt was always trying to paint me as this helpless heiress who was flighty. The reality was I had supported us as a copywriter during the last two years of our marriage. And while my parents were well off, they weren't so well off they could simply give me money to stay home and take care of our kids. They were willing to pay tuition, but that was it. I needed to work.

But Matt was never practical. He was determined to have us move to the North Shore. And it didn't matter what he had to do to make it happen. So, with his attorney's help, he began making me out to be a terrible mother so the decision would be his, not mine.

His only issue was that I wasn't a bad mother. I didn't hit my kids or drink around them. They were well-fed and, most importantly, well-loved. But I had made one fatal mistake. After the divorce, I became involved with a preppy con man who robbed me of my self-esteem and jewelry I had inherited from my grandmothers. He was a criminal in corduroy and Nantucket red sail pants. Who I was, what I tolerated, and how I put myself and my children in danger are things I will never forgive myself for. Being forty, suddenly on my own with a disturbing quiet, was more than I could bear. Enter this man. I never say his name. We met at a party. He was tall, blond, with a deep voice. He was everything my high school self had wanted. He had friends who owned property where we vacationed in the summer, his parents had a place in the same community where my grandparents had lived in the winter, and he was charming and had a powerful sexual draw. I was hooked.

As with what Jung would call a Demon Lover, the affair was amazing for six weeks. Even though the night we met, a small voice said, "You don't have to do this," I ignored it. Being with him felt like being addicted to drugs. We would talk for hours on the phone about everything: all my problems, what I wanted from my life. We would laugh. After years of being completely ignored by my ex, having someone be attentive to my every thought felt like rain on a hot day. Like I was being nourished and seen. Initially, he introduced me to his friends, we went out together and talked about our future. And I felt normal for the first time in a long time. I completely isolated myself during my marriage's demise because of work and financial stress. My life had been in complete chaos, and I felt used. I didn't have any extra energy for normal interactions. When my marriage was finally over, I felt like I had been at war.

The con man gave me a lie that felt like love. He told me I was beautiful, that he loved me. He listened to my stories and seemed to understand the weird WASP world I came from. But like the character of the Devil in John Irving's, *The Witches of Eastwick*, these conversations were not about connections but gathering information to be used against me later. He was studying me as he studied all his victims. He only came by when my kids were with their dad. We would have sex that would last for hours, and then he would leave. Later, I would learn that predators are constantly scanning their interactions with people to find potential victims. Because of my insecurities and isolation, I was an easy target.

Then, on a dime, it changed.

He was less available. He didn't make time to have dinner or introduce me to his friends anymore. Finally, we "broke up." It didn't matter. I was still obsessed with him. So began an excruciating four-year period in which we would occasionally hook up. Like a gambler, I was chasing that first high of connection each time, hoping that things would change. He knew what I wanted. He would fill my head with hope. Hope that I was desirable and powerful and that I wouldn't be alone. The reality of my life was that I struggled with being a single parent, having a job, and ultimately feeling lonely and anonymous.

His affection had felt like a portal back to my youth. When I was part of a civilization of families in which men wore blue sports coats, I had an arsenal of cocktail dresses, homes were tastefully decorated with grass-cloth and antiques, and there existed a silent but codified set of rules and boundaries. Where the people I knew, our families had known each other for generations. Who their cousins were, and where they had grown up. Where I felt part of a continuum of context; although I never felt entirely accepted by those people, it felt somehow like my natural habitat. In contrast, Chicago felt like the wilderness. I felt like I was always starting over from a deficit. And my subconscious couldn't reconcile that, so when I met him, it seemed like a chance to return to my prior life. I placed myself in a cult of my own making, anointing him as the cult leader.

I always knew he was lying. About having a job. About where he went to school. About how much money he had. He was always drinking and forever moving from one shitty, temporary apartment to another under the guise of looking for the right house. There was always a crazy girl after him. The women weren't crazy, simply angry because he had lied to them. Everything came to a head one morning when I discovered my jewelry was gone. I was going to a family wedding and wanted to wear some of the pieces. I remember opening up the drawer, looking through each velvet box, and finding the ring that was promised to me from childhood gone, earrings, a diamond ring that had been my great-grandmother's, the Cartier gold bracelet M. had gotten me on our honeymoon in Paris. Gone. Like dry ice on skin cancer or realizing you have wet your pants in public, seeing their empty boxes was so painful and shameful it physically burned.

I instantly knew he had taken every last piece when I was getting coffee in the morning. Finally, like a thunderclap, the fever was broken. I went to the police. They ignored me. I confronted him. That yielded nothing. I partnered up with another victim; the police didn't believe us. They thought we were jealous ex-girlfriends. During this time, unfortunately, my ex-husband heard about the whole event. He tucked this information away, like a weapon, waiting for the right time to use it. And taking our daughters from me was that moment he chose.

The months leading up to court were surreal. First, M. and I had to pay for a court advocate to investigate the school I wanted to send our daughter to. I found out later that the court advocate shared office space with M.'s attorney's father. This relationship seemed like a conflict of interest, plus he was expensive. When he interviewed me, he came across as the most concerned man for children ever. He had a mustache and salt-and-pepper hair. He shared the story of his daughter with learning disabilities. And how proud of her he was. He was full of it.

He investigated the school and looked into the services of the Wilmette school district. Ultimately, he sided with me, but not before saying he needed more money because he had spent so much time on this case. My winning made M. even angrier because it cost him more money. He didn't give up. That's when his lawyer sent over a poorly written brief postulating that because I had been in a relationship with a criminal, I had shown lousy judgment and, therefore, I shouldn't be allowed to make decisions about the girls. I felt like I'd been caught. I was fueled by righteous anger, but now I was on my heels. I was a bad mother and a fool. What kind of person gets involved with someone so vile? For years, I imagined myself to be a strong, courageous woman. But my parents were paying my legal fees and the private school education for my kids. Maybe M. was right. Maybe I was a spoiled debutante.

I can't remember how long it took us to get to court. Months, minutes. Sometimes, I feel like I am still there, in an antechamber of fear and self-loathing. I prayed and asked my personal deities, as well as some impersonal ones, for strength and protection for myself and my children. Finally, the court day came. After a sleepless night, I got dressed and steeled myself.

"How are you doing?" asked the senior partner when I arrived at the courthouse.

She was an older woman, a widow, who seemed to know everything and everyone. Debra only came around when things were serious. Debra was seasoned and knew the nuances of the judges and the other attorneys. One of the most important things I learned from being in divorce court was that it was a small, contained universe. All the judges and lawyers knew each other well. There was no dramatic winning or losing. The contours of the cases seemed to be decided well before court even started; today seemed different.

I noticed M.'s attorney was getting help from his father, a legendary divorce attorney. He must have been really nervous about the hearing, or he would not have brought his daddy to court. That gave me a sliver of hope.

We waited outside the courtroom. There was some good news already: Our usual judge was not on the docket. He wasn't exactly sexist, but he was pretty lenient with M. We all entered the courtroom. The judge was a petite but serious looking African American woman. M.'s lawyer went up to the bench and handed her a piece of paper.

"He wants a different judge," Debra whispered in my ear.

I could see why. This woman felt like she may be sympathetic to my case. Perhaps the universe was judging me less harshly than I was judging myself. Next, we waited for another judge to become available. It seemed like forever. Fear kept creeping in, but I pushed it away. I had made a mistake. A terrible one, but I was right to fight for my girls, for myself. Finally, another judge became available. We walked into her courtroom. Unlike the other one, which had a more modern and nondescript feature, this one had deep, cherry-looking panels. It looked like a courtroom on TV. The judge was not there.

A man came out, and my lawyers and M.'s were ushered back through a door. Before my younger attorney left, he said, "Don't talk to him." M. and I were left alone. We didn't speak. M. stood up and had a rolled-up piece of paper he kept hitting his hand with while he glared at me. I simply stared back. This wasn't about the girls. This was about him wanting to show me and the world that he had been wronged, that, despite everything M. had done, he was the injured party.

It seemed like we waited forever, like there was a ticking clock in my psyche. Besides being angry, M.'s eyes looked panicked, like a wounded animal. I kept wondering what was taking so long. The amount of focus I had had all day felt like I was taking my SATs, except the result would not be getting into college but keeping my life.

At last, the door opened, and my lawyers stuck their heads out and motioned me into a hallway.

"You won," they said, smiling with satisfaction.

"How? She didn't even come out of chambers?"

"She looked over the filing and said the case was ridiculous; this woman isn't a bad mother."

I couldn't believe it. After months of fear, self-doubt, and marinating in shame, a woman I hadn't even met judged me to be a good mother.

***

Anne Wagner is a creative director and copywriter who resides in the Andersonville neighborhood of Chicago. She is mother to two grown daughters and a rescue pup, Rosy. Anne is a volunteer, avid reader, and is working on her first novel.

9 | The Promise Made by Sherrill Bodine

The late summer sun blazed down, prickling along my skin and heating my palm, which was enveloped by Mom's larger hand, her fingers curled tight around mine. She squinted her eyes against the glare and sang out in the still heavy air. "Step on a crack, break your mother's back, step on a crack, break your mother's back."

I mirrored her as we hopped over the narrow breaks on the cement sidewalk between our wide roofless, front porch and the gravel shoulder running along Earl Avenue. Our house stood on the last street in Lafayette, Indiana before the factory and the corn fields stretched to the horizon.

It sounded like a crack of thunder as the front door of our house opened and slammed shut.

My Aunt Marge hurried down the porch steps toward us. In the white glare, her blue-green eyes sparkled and her curly burnished hair, lit with sun brightened red streaks, streamed out behind her.

She laughed as she clasped our hands, swinging us around in a circle. "Gwennie, I'll play with you. Sherrill needs to go help in the kitchen. Okay?"

Mom let go of my hand. "Hurry and come right back, Sherrill Lynn. I want to play some more."

Why did they want only me? Mom and I were always together.

The heat from the boiling pots on the stove and the sweet smell of simmering peaches and cinnamon filled the kitchen. Steam hung like angel halos above Granny's and Grandma's heads.

I rubbed my thumb nail over and over my upper lip, like I always did when I felt confused or afraid. "Did I do something wrong?"

"Nothing wrong." My great-granny Buckles sank down on a chair at the kitchen table to fuss with the big, white lopsided bun of hair at the back of her small head. "Something important your grandma and I need to talk to you about now that you are five and asking so many questions."

I stopped rubbing my lip to gaze up at Grandma.

"Sherrill, you need to know that Doc Cox and all of us thought your mother was the most beautiful and sweet baby from the day she was born. You know Doc Cox. He makes house calls when we're sick."

I remembered the grey-haired man carrying a big black bag. "He came when I had the measles. He gave me two suckers. Mom, too."

"That's right. He told us that your mom wasn't right."

My hand shook, heading to my lip for comfort. "What do you mean? Are you sick, Grandma? Is Mom sick and is Doc Cox coming back to make her right again?"

"I'm fine, but your mom isn't." She sucked in a long, deep breath and seemed to grow even taller, so I had to lean back to see her face.

"Not right means your mom wasn't born smart, like your uncles and aunt. She's different from most other people. Some might even say she's bad different if they saw her having one of her spells."

Heat from the boiling pots flushed through my body, burning my skin, drenching my eyes with tears. "I don't like you saying Mom's bad! Take it back!"

Grandma fell to her knees in front of me and her eyes glistened like glass. "I know you don't understand how your mom is different. I know to you, she's a full-grown woman like me and Granny. But … but inside, she's a little girl, like you, and she always will be. Already you're smarter than your mom. You're going to start noticing how people act around her. They might even say things about her that are mean, and you need to understand why. And … and they might say things about you. But you must never listen to that or let it make you sad."

I didn't want to hear the confusing words she was saying. I wanted to go play with Mom like I did every day for as long as I could remember.

"Sherrill, please listen. You need to know it isn't your mom's fault she can't read and write or understand things like you do. You need to know that when she yells and does scary things, it isn't her fault."

"Not her fault." Granny patted tears away from her rosy cheeks. "Our Good Lord made a mistake when He created your mom."

Grandma sank back on her heels. "We tried to give your mom the life she would have had if she'd been born right, like your Uncle Bob, Uncle Ed, and Aunt Marge. We gave her lots of love and protected her against people calling her cruel words like … stupid … or idiot … or … retard. You must learn these are terrible words that no one should ever use."

"We did what we believed best to make everything right for your mother and our Good Lord rewarded us with you." Granny's voice echoed through the hot air. "Now, through you, she will have the family and everything she should have had. Do you understand what we are asking you to do?"

In that split second, the journey my family had forged for me before I was born began.

"I don't understand, but I'll do it!" I shouted the words above the hissing pots and the sound of Granny's sobs.

She nodded. "I believe you. Now go back and play with your mom. That's what makes her happy. Don't you worry. We'll sort things out soon enough."

"I'll find mom right now and start fixing her!" The words surging through me, filling me with a scary, powerful excitement. I fled the kitchen.

But I got only as far as the living room. My grandpa was waiting for me. He pushed his brown felt hat to the back of his head as his soft blue eyes, kind like Granny's, watched me.

"Sherri, don't be scared. I know you learned a lot of family secrets today. It'd be best for your mom if you never talk to others about what you were told about her not being right. And you must never tell her she isn't right. It would hurt her."

"When I fix Mom, will my dad come live with us like Uncle Bob does with Linda and Uncle Ed does with Gary and Brian?"

He turned away to stare through the narrow front windows. "Best not to talk about that right now. Don't look good outside. Go on now and play while I find out what's happenin'."

"Something is brewing," Granny called from the open front door behind me. "The air is too still. Like the wind is holding its breath. We all need to be inside."

"Sherrill, bring your mom," Aunt Marge shouted, running ahead of Granny, who ushered us into the kitchen, where Grandma stood staring out the windows.

I inched closer to Grandpa, hunkering over the radio. It crackled with static every time he twisted the dial. "What's the matter, Grandpa?"

A strange beeping filled the room and a hollow voice repeated, "Weather Alert! Weather Alert! A tornado has touched down in Tippecanoe County. A second tornado has touched down north of Lafayette, Indiana. People in the vicinity should seek shelter immediately!"

Grandpa jumped up. "Marge, take everyone to the basement. Maude, open some windows so the house won't implode."

Grandma rushed around the room to push open windows and turn off the stove.

I ached to rub my lip, but my fingers were wound too tight with Mom's.

Aunt Marge grabbed my free hand. "You and your mom need to come with me to Granny's room."

Fear turned my legs numb, and I froze to the floor.

"Hurry up, Sherrill. Move!" Aunt Marge pulled us, and I fought free to stumble one numb step, then two, forcing my heavy feet to shuffle through the dining room into Granny's bedroom.

Aunt Marge pushed away the white wicker screen and flung open the ugly, ancient gray door. "C'mon! Quick! Go down!"

Mom reared back, pulling me with her, away from the rickety wooden stairway leading into our dirt basement. "Don't like it down there in the cellar. It's dirty and got bugs everywhere. Sherrill ain't ever going down there. Me either."

"You need to go now, Gwennie." Again, Aunt Marge pulled us toward the open door.

I looked at mom. "We gotta do what Aunt Marge says. Tornados are really bad. We have to hide from them."

"Listen to Sherrill, Gwennie. We need to hide. Not all the way down. Only to the second step."

Her face pale, her eyes shifting between me and the door, Mom began to cry.

Granny gently urged us, and I pressed against Mom to inch her toward the door. "Don't be scared. I'm right beside you."

I shifted her, and Granny kept gently pushing at our backs until we were squeezed together on the steps above the damp-smelling dirt floor.

Grandpa stepped inside, slammed the door, and gripped the handle, holding it closed against the scary thing on the other side.

The wind stopped holding its breath. It whistled and moaned against the trembling door in Grandpa's clenched fists.

"No need to fear. The Good Lord will keep us safe." Granny nodded so hard her white hair tumbled out of her bun to tickle my cheek.

Stories flashed through my head. "The tornado won't take our house into the sky the way it did Dorothy's in that book you read to Mom and me, right, Granny?"

"Don't want to fly into the sky," Mom cried, shivering beside me.

I wrapped myself around her arm. "Granny never tells fibs, Mom. We'll be safe and I'm here to protect you. Like the Lion, and the Tin Man and Scarecrow did for Dorothy, remember?"

"Good one, Sherrill." Aunt Marge glanced over her shoulder and smiled. "I swear you're five going on twenty."

"Amen on that." Granny sighed. "And praise the Lord. The wind has slowed. This is simply a bad storm. Listen to that rain."

When the siren wailed all clear, we scrambled up the steps to watch the fierce rain pound against our long front windows and the ground until our cracked sidewalk disappeared under water. It splashed over the rim of the porch, like a lake growing bigger and bigger out into the street. The rain went on all day and the lake grew deeper and wider until it came into our house, muddy water inching higher in our basement.

"Need to save what we can," Grandpa shouted as he rushed down the rickety steps.

Dripping mud on Granny's wood floor, Grandpa carried up boxes, handing them off to Grandma and Aunt Marge until the water reached the steps, where we'd been safe from the wind.

"Got all I could." He dropped the last box at our feet.

Mom squealed. "Look, Sherrill Lynn. These are the comic books about vampires and werewolves my brother Ed used to read to me. Remember, Mom?"

Grandma looked up from where she and Aunt Marge were crawling across the floor, mopping up muddy water with rags. "Sure do remember. Sherrill, why don't you go upstairs to your mom's room and read these to her while we clean up this mess."

Besides the old, battered gray door to the basement, the only room in our house with anything besides a curtain hung to cover the opening was Mom's bedroom, with its plastic accordion barrier. Inside, on every surface and covering all the walls, were treasures brought to her by everyone who visited our house. Mom slid closed the door to lock us in. This was our special place, off limits to everyone, family, and visitors alike. One by one, she placed the comic books in rows across her pink and white quilted bedspread.

"Here, Sherrill Lynn, read this one first." She thrust a comic into my hands.

My eyes fixed on pictures of monsters with sharp teeth dripping blood. I studied the pages and tried to understand words so unlike any in my Dick and Jane reader.

"The vampires are the ones who come out at night to suck our blood, right? How can the moon turn men into wolves?"

Mom leaned closer, and I felt her breath hot on my neck. "My cousin Ivernell told me vampires and werewolves are real and can turn us into them. They come get us at night. But I won't never let nothing bad happen to you. You're all I got. I love you, Sherrill Lynn."

I didn't understand about monsters in the night, but I understood the great rush of emotion my mother inspired in me. I hugged her tight, just as she liked, and kissed both her cheeks over and over until she giggled, her lips softening into a smile.

"Don't you worry, Mom. I promise I'll find a way nothing bad ever happens to you."

As promised, Granny came upstairs to help Mom tuck me into my cot on the landing outside her bedroom door.

I glanced out the low window beside my bed at the moonlight glittering on wide puddles of water in our front yard. "I figured out how to keep the vampires away by making crosses, but I don't know what I should do to keep Mom safe from werewolves, Granny. Do you know what I should do?"

"Our Good Lord knows how to keep you both from danger. Just as he knew to give your mother the very best daughter in you."

Mom clapped her hands. "Sherrill Lynn's the bestest daughter in the whole world, ain't she, Granny?"

"Yes, Gwen. I believe she is indeed."

To keep my promise, I needed to always be the best daughter in the whole world. Granny had told me it was the reason I was born.

I believed her.

Abridged First Chapter of her forthcoming memoir, *I, Warrior*.

***

Sherrill Bodine is the author of eighteen published novels from Harlequin, Fawcett Regency, and Grand Central. Plus, she's written numerous travel articles for *Go World Travel*. *I, Warrior* is her first non-fiction book.

She is proud to serve on several charity boards in the Chicago area when she is not traveling the world.

Please follow her on FB, Instagram, her blog, Bigbiggerbiggest.life and YouTube channel, *Dare to be Curious* for fun, fashion, books and stories of modern heroines.

10 | Genetic Markers by Madeleine Holden

I remember when I was six years old, my dad used to say that I was born under a lucky star. At my birthday party that year, my mother said, "Make a wish." My wish was a statement. "I am going to have a baby." I made a wish on a lucky star that sometime in my life I would be a mother. Deep down, I knew this was the truth.

Some of my friends were obsessed with the man, the wedding day, the plan. I never thought about that. I thought boys were good to outrun and play soccer with. Others were obsessed with the sex they were going to have with men: their Barbie and Ken dolls became porn stars. Later, as a teenager, I thought the worst thing in life would be to get pregnant by accident and disappoint my parents. I muddled through birth control and my own messy teenage relationships with little guidance, largely keeping to myself for fear of revealing I did not know what I was doing.

There was worse, though. I became paralyzed at eighteen, hit by a car in a dangerous situation. I woke up after three weeks in a drug-induced coma in the hospital, confused with little memory of what happened.

"My name is Doctor Moore," a figure in the semi-darkness said beside my bed. "I am your neurosurgeon. I have restabilized your neck, and the operation went well. We will have to wait for the swelling to go down in your spinal cord to determine the level of upper-body movement you will have to work with." And then he took a deep breath and said, "You will not walk again."

I felt like I was in a bad movie, cast in the wrong role. He tried a positive spin saying, "I know this is not the life you expected, but you could continue with your education, learn to drive, have a family."

I had been hallucinating on medications and was struggling with reality. I wondered if this was just another nightmare, or if this doctor was crazy. Who would ever choose me as a life partner now? How could I ever be a mother without moving? He was trying to give hope, but it was ludicrous. I was devastated and could not imagine what my purpose in life could be if I couldn't be a mother, the only thing I ever really wanted. The darkness overwhelmed me. I remember one orderly waking me in the middle of the night, asking why I was crying. I had been fast asleep, weeping, my despair and grief so deep it carried into my unconsciousness, floating through my dreams.

"What will you miss the most?" he asked sincerely, leaning in with his hands on the bars of my bed.

"Well, walking on the beach, I think. I used to love the feeling of the waves splashing up my legs and finding little treasures," I replied through my tears.

In our nightly talks, I realized how much more was lost for me forever. "I used to play the piano, you know, and ski and skate and swim. I can't imagine a life of sitting still."

Living was a daily struggle in rehab. I was so weak, so vulnerable. I got a second deep-vein thrombosis in my leg, caught every infection that flowed freely in my ward, and was sent to the ER when my lips turned blue from lack of oxygen. Sometimes, I thought death was the only answer. No one person could endure so much.

Then I met Jane. She was my physiotherapist in rehab, a young woman in her thirties, with long black hair and kind eyes. Every day, for an hour over the course of a year, I was transferred to her big blue mat, and we pushed through the pain of my physical injuries. She would touch my shoulder, my back, my neck, and I could feel the heat from her hands flowing into my body. Our energy joined, healing my broken parts.

When Jane got pregnant with her partner, I watched her belly grow. With my leg in her hands, her body pushing down on my bent knee to keep the flexibility in my hip, I confided in her. "You're very lucky to be having a baby. I always wanted to have one," I said.

Jane was quiet and then said, "You probably still can, but you're going to get some resistance."

My time with Jane helped me analyze the whirlwind my life had become. Everything was happening all at once: adapting a van so it was wheelchair friendly, renovating my parents' home so I could get out on weekends. I was also securing old friendships and making new ones, accepting the permanence of my disability. It was exciting and terrifying. Throughout this time, Jane grounded me on that mat.

One day, we were talking about sexuality. I was so uncomfortable in my new skin and wondered if I would even feel physical pleasure again. A friend of mine had offered to spend his life with me and have children with me as a favor. I wondered if I was asking too much out of life and should settle for a lifetime of companionship, but I wanted more and I didn't think I needed charity.

Jane adamantly said, "Don't settle. You deserve more than that."

We discussed our fathers and what roles they played in raising us. I told her how my father would brush the knots out of my long blond hair after a bath, that he helped me with science and math homework and taught me to swim, skate, and ski. We agreed active fathers should just be normal expected behavior for men. Jane reminded me that African women say it takes a village to raise a child. I laughed, but wanted to cry as I would need a whole tribe to make this work, not just an active partner.

Another day, we were discussing labor, and I wondered if I could deliver naturally or would have to have a caesarean because of paralysis. Jane said she had seen both occur in previous clients. She told me about other women and their experiences, how each injury healed differently, making it impossible to know what would happen to me.

When Jane left to have her baby, I confided in a nurse practitioner at a family clinic that I hoped to have children one day. Her face turned crimson as her eyes filled with water. She put a forced smile on her face and just looked at me in horror.

I said, "What do you think? I also plan to breastfeed if I can. Women with a high spinal cord injury have done it before."

"You won't lactate. Your body's dead below your injury."

I was saddened by her reaction, coming from a professional whom I respected and liked after years of care. I recall sitting in the waiting room trying to make sense of what she had said. My body was not dead below the injury. I breathed air, ate, drank, and digested. My body sustained me, carried my brain, my heart, my soul. She was wrong. I thought of the resistance Jane had mentioned. Then, I was called in to see the doctor.

The doctor was a middle-aged man with a stern gaze. He sat behind his commanding desk and waited for me to begin. I nervously stammered as I explained I hoped to have children one day and wondered if there was a reason I couldn't. It was as if I was seeking permission or approval, terrified of making another life-changing mistake.

"Well, some of these medications might be a problem," he said, staring at my file, refusing to make eye contact. Before I could ask which medications and why, he went on. "You know, I have a friend in a wheelchair who drives a van and became a doctor." Before I knew it, I was in the hallway, my questions unanswered, frustrated that I was being sidelined. He seemed to communicate that a disabled woman could not or should not want to have a child.

But then the universe conspired in my favor. I was encouraged to choose my own topics for research projects in the social work program at McGill University. This allowed me to delve deeply into pertinent topics for me and my peers in the disabled community. I explored disability and body image, disability and the health care system, and mothers with disabilities. My professors were impressed with the depth of my research and the authenticity of my work. They invited me to speak in rehabilitation centers and to women's rights groups. I thrived in this academic environment and my confidence grew.

And then I fell in love. My carpenter friend, who had custody of his twin two-year-old boys, became my lover and partner. The twins were hungry for stories and knowledge, and so was I. We grew close and taught each other. Embracing the surprise of the stepmother role, I was grateful and curious. I wondered how much of my nurturing would affect the men they would become and how much biology dictated.

One day, in a battle of wills, one twin faced me, fists clenched at his sides, hurling words meant to hurt me, but only revealing his own pain. "You are not my mother!"

I responded gently with the only possible answer, "I know."

I still wanted to become pregnant, so I met with my hematologist. She leaned up against her desk and crossed her arms. I worried about what she might say.

She looked directly at me. "You have all the working organs. You're not sick. You're paralyzed. Here's what you must do. Because of the anticoagulant you take to prevent blood clots, you must know very early when you are pregnant because the brain starts to develop first in the sixth week. You must count your days. You must be smart. On the fifth day, if you're late, stop taking that medication, and test if you're pregnant. When we are sure that you're pregnant, we will start injecting you with something else for the nine months to keep you and your baby healthy. We will follow you at the at-risk clinic."

"So, it's safe?" I asked.

"It is as safe for you as any other woman," she answered.

My shoulders relaxed. I breathed deeply. After ten years, I finally got an honest answer, intelligent, with facts, given without judgement about social norms and prescribed expectations of the mothering role. I had waded through a murky topic, where information was difficult to find and questions were impossible to answer. Just a generation before, many people with disabilities didn't survive, were institutionalized for life, even sterilized. Society was changing, and I had a role to play in that.

I was impatient to expand my family, but as much as I wanted to control the situation, I was repeatedly disappointed. Month after month, I wasn't becoming pregnant. Perhaps I had been infertile all along, so I consulted a physician. When the doctor asked me if I wanted to increase my chances with hormones and other ways, I gave up. I had been counting my days religiously, having sex at peak fertile moments. If it was meant to happen, it would, I thought as I let the tears flow in the van on the way home.

And then it did, just like magic.

Everything unfolded in perfect, miraculous timing. My ideal family manifested; a man who had been caring for his twins long before I ever appeared in their lives, someone looking for a partner in life, twins old enough to help with a baby sometimes, a supportive social network of family and friends, and good health. I had changed from a person who kept her questions to herself to one who openly and publicly questioned everything. I triumphed over impossible odds, found my voice, and built my tribe. I was blessed many times over. And I got to be a mother.

Thirty years later, it was a Sunday. It was going to be a beautiful day. This wet July, the skies were heavy with the smoke of uncontrolled forest fires in northern Quebec. But on this day, the skies were blue, and I could see clearly. One twin was coming with his wife and daughter, our very first grandchild. We sat in the backyard at the picnic table soaking up the sun, watching her splash around in a little plastic pool I got for her. Our eyes told her we love

66

her, and I imagined her feeling the way I did, looking at my cake, making a wish, showered in love. When I looked at her blonde hair and blue eyes, I recalled long ago having the little twin boys sitting on my lap and reading stories to them. Two boys I loved and taught as if they were my own, before I had my three children, each one so different, even identical twins. I loved them all so much I thought my heart would burst. And my heart once again overflowed for my granddaughter as she danced, laughed, and played that day.

I thought I had lost everything I had ever wanted in an accident at eighteen, and yet, in a very roundabout way, I triumphed in the end.

***

Madeleine Holden is a storyteller and author. She has performed for Bodies of Stories, Soul Stories Live, Confabulation in Montreal, and at the Toronto International Storytelling Festival. She has been featured on several podcasts: *The Volume Knob—The Songs that Saved Your Life* and *NAMI North Carolina*. Her story, "A Loving Spirit," was published in *Storytellers` True Stories about Love, Volume 1*.

Madeleine lives in St. Isidore, Quebec, with her husband, where she studies, reads, and writes her memoir stories.

11 | Our Own Definition of Triumph by Barbara Apelian Beall

I sensed that the news would not be good when the thoracic surgeon cleared the small waiting area, sat down across from me, and reached for my hand.

He calmly said, "I am so sorry to tell you that your husband has advanced lung cancer and the pleural effusion, the fluid that built up in his lungs, indicates the cancer has spread. I put in a chest tube, and he should breathe much better now."

He then asked me if I understood what he said. I could repeat his words, but I could not wrap my head or my heart around what they meant.

He continued, "I know this is a great deal of information to take in, but there is a social worker and other resources to help you both. Your husband likely has three months or so given the progression of the cancer. My advice is to get your affairs in order and live your lives in the time you have together."

And then I was alone. No tears, just a stunned silence. Frankly, if you had told me that little green men had landed from Mars, it would have been easier to believe than the diagnosis and the dismal prognosis of only three months. My husband, Herb, never smoked. He was a long-distance runner, heading out each lunch hour with his running group at the university.

Get our affairs in order? This was my husband, the man I loved and planned to grow old with. We had planned our retirement together. How did we come to this? The discovery of the cancer began when he came home early from running a race several days earlier.

Herb said, "I won my race, but my time was so slow I was embarrassed to have it announced. I just couldn't seem to get my breath."

I was headed off to a conference the next morning, and he promised to call our doctor's office. When I returned, he had an inhaler and said that a resident had ordered an X-ray and said his lungs looked clear. But he had a dry, deep cough. Things changed quickly and later that night he struggled to breathe. He looked alarmed, gasping for breath, and admitted he was in pain.

By 11 p.m. that night, we were in the Emergency Room. While they ran tests, I read Shakespeare's Otello aloud to him, playing all the parts. Reading in the most even, soothing voice that I could manage gave us both a sense of calm. I paused for the bloodwork, X-rays, and all the questions. Many hours later, they determined he had a pleural effusion in the tissues lining his lungs. The list of candidates causing this were pneumonia, congestive heart failure, cancer, and a pulmonary embolism. I was not thrilled with any of those diagnoses, but prayed for pneumonia. At least that could be knocked out with antibiotics.

The surgeon said he had to put a chest tube into Herb's lungs to drain the fluid, and the surgery was scheduled for early that morning. After the surgical procedure, we learned he had stage four cancer.

After his diagnosis, Herb stayed in the hospital for a week. We were overwhelmed with all the doctors, nurses, and social workers dispensing information and counsel. I reeled with so much to process in a brief period. There was the cancer, the horrific news to share with family and friends, the possible treatment options, the upcoming medical appointments, and facing a life without him.

Family, friends, and our minister came to the hospital. At one point, Herb's running group ran over to the hospital during their lunch hour. When I came to visit, there were ten sweaty runners gathered around his bed holding hands, led in prayer by our minister. I smiled at the oddity of the situation, sensing their love for Herb.

Herb tried to be positive and realistic. When a friend offered to bring a meal, he quickly responded, "I'd like a cheeseburger, French fries, and fried onion rings because I don't have to worry about my cholesterol level anymore! The cancer will get me first!"

I seesawed between feeling terribly alone and wonderfully supported. The devastating news had leveled us emotionally, but we were buoyed by the love and caring of our children, their families, extended family, and friends who called us. We were touched by how many people came to visit and by all the people who said they would pray for us at their churches.

Our oldest daughter flew out from Chicago and the three of us listened to treatment options. Together, we chose participation in an experimental chemotherapy treatment and sealed our decision with a group hug. Perhaps we could beat the three-month prognosis.

When Herb was discharged, we saw our lawyer, our financial advisor, and our accountant. Things were "in order" and we consciously re-booted our lives. At times, I felt that I was clawing my way back into a rhythm of normality. We measured time in a new way—BC (before cancer) and AC (after cancer)—but we decided to live our lives as fully as possible despite the treatments and the realization of the certainty of death. We refused to wear only the appellations of cancer patient and cancer patient's wife. Herb had so many other roles that defined him. I too had many roles, with the most recent being an organizer of appointments and dispenser of updates on his condition. I wondered how I would juggle my many roles, when the role I wanted most was to be his wife.

Friends from his running group joined him on the track to race walk so he could keep in good physical condition. And although his serious running days were in the past, months later, Herb ran the last mile with our two older daughters as they crossed the finish line at the Chicago marathon. It brought tears to all our eyes.

The experimental chemotherapy treatment we opted for shrunk the tumor in his lungs, but not for all in the test group. One young man whom Herb liked died within months.

He told me in a quavering voice, "Barbara, he was only twenty-four with a wife and new baby. He hoped the treatments would give him more time, but he died yesterday."

While others in the test group died, my husband lived on. Ironically, his lungs were strong, helped by his years as a runner. Herb was living in the present and in some ways preparing to die by carefully selecting projects to complete and allocating time for loved ones. I too was living in the present, savoring the time we had together. However, I was also preparing for life without him. It was a delicate balance that sometimes left me feeling exhausted as well as guilty. I told a friend and mentor at my university that lecturing in my classes provided a welcomed relief from the pressures of the management and decisions linked to cancer treatments. She kindly responded, "Barbara, you too need to care for yourself and to take part in your present and your future. And you have a responsibility to do so."

After months of treatment, Herb was in remission. We had no idea how long it might last, but we saw this as an opportunity because we were no longer constantly tethered to hospital appointments.

Elated with the news, I turned to him. "What do you want to do with this gift of time?"

Herb responded immediately with a huge smile, "See our children and grandchildren. And you and I need to make one more trip to England together."

Our desire to go to England was because his mother had lived in East Sussex for many years, and we had visited annually, spending time in her idyllic 350-year-old country cottage. Walking up the brick path leading to the front door, we enjoyed the scent of the many-colored roses growing up the trellis on the small brick cottage. We often hiked for days on the Cotswold Way and the South Downs Way, through fields, over stiles and stopping at charming villages for meals and overnight stays.

But for this trip, we decided to spend the week in London. Holding hands as we landed at Heathrow Airport, I mused, "I never thought we would get a chance to have another trip to England together!"

He smiled at me and said, "We have a week to enjoy and explore the city together."

We headed to our hotel in Kensington, which was near an underground station. Herb had a lifelong love of trains, and he loved riding the tube. He knew the map of the London subway system and proudly told me about some of the history of the stations. Even mundane things like riding the tube was fun with him, and we did it three or four times every day.

Our first night in London, we looked at each other as the dinner hour approached, and said at the same time, "Indian food," so off we went to the restaurant nearby. At dinner we toasted the gift of time. We were living in the moment, and that moment was glorious.

In the following days, we toured the Victoria and Albert Museum and The National Gallery. One afternoon, we went to the well-known Fortnum and Mason, where we enjoyed tea with scones, clotted cream, and strawberry jam. At Liberty of London, we bought a new blue and red tie for him and a silk scarf for me. We wore them throughout our stay. We also stopped at Harrod's food market, where we enjoyed tasting cheeses and even a boar pate.

A couple of days before we were supposed to leave, I awakened to hear Herb coughing. I knew that cough and I felt a chill go through me. It was the dry cough that first alerted us that something was wrong. In the morning, he called his oncologist to make an appointment for the day after we flew home.

He turned to me with a sad expression and said, "It's back, but let's not spoil the rest of our time together."

I hugged him and wanted to scream at the injustice of the diagnosis and the return of the cancer. I wanted more time, always more time. We cried together.

When we arrived back in the United States, Herb underwent a different chemotherapy treatment, but the results were grim. The cancer had metastasized to his brain. Despite the potential risks of plane travel, we flew to Oregon, where our youngest daughter gave birth to her first child. In a house filled with the robust cries of our new grandson, Herb said, "I volunteer to hold him when he fusses. I have plenty of energy for that." And so he became the chief babysitter.

After a couple of weeks, we flew back to Boston in time to see the 4th of July parade in Rockport highlighted by a marching group known for taking beach chairs and folding and unfolding them in unison. It was a hilarious part of the community.

"Can you imagine this happening anywhere else with such flare?" he said and laughed. His sense of humor never diminished during the entire time he was sick.

We were soon back at the hospital, taking in more information. Given that the cancer had metastasized extensively, we opted to end treatments and continue only palliative care at home. The last few months of his life were both a blessing and a curse. I painfully watched Herb's physical strength decline but, mercifully, his cognitive abilities remained. At night, I would climb into his hospital bed until he slept. Lying beside him, I wanted to memorize every contour of his body and the sound of his breathing, anticipating when he was no longer with me.

We filled the next couple of months with visits from our daughters, their families, and close friends. We celebrated his sixty-fourth birthday with cake and a huge bouquet of balloons.

When asked what he wanted for his special meal, Herb said, "That red wine I had always enjoyed, corn bread, and lobster." We organized the eclectic meal. A dear friend first checked all the liquor stores in the area and then called her clients, who had wine collections, and found that rare wine. She also brought over lobster, and because he was weak, she fed him. A couple living across the way made corn bread for us all. It was a grand birthday.

I would like to say that there was a miracle and that my husband was cured, but with metastatic lung cancer that was not to be, and we knew that from the beginning. On August thirty-first, we woke to a glorious morning with a cool breeze from the ocean. Herb had fallen into a coma the night before, and his breathing was erratic. Through tears, I thanked him for a wonderful life and told him I loved him. I would miss him, but it was time for him to go. He died in my arms. It was three years and ten months after his diagnosis.

Although so many with cancer and their families talk about their "fight" or "battle," it seems to make their deaths sound as if they lost or somehow failed. But for many, death from cancer is an inevitability. Cancer was listed on my husband's death certificate as the cause of death, but it did not define the entirety of his life or our lives together. We continued to live and to love post diagnosis and that was our triumph.

***

Barbara Apelian Beall debuts as a memoir writer in this volume. She is a Professor Emerita of the History of Art at Assumption University and after retirement was a Visiting Professor at Clark University. She has published books and articles on a variety of subjects. Living in the rural, northern Berkshires has given her the opportunity to reflect upon her life. She thanks the editors at Chicago Story Press who have shepherded her through this experience.

12 | The Resiliency I Didn't Know I Have by Linda Strader

Over the years, people have often told me I am resilient—a true survivor. To be honest, I questioned their assessment, and sometimes adamantly disagreed. I believed that most everyone would have done what I did.

After graduating high school in 1973, I struggled to find suitable employment. When I say suitable, I mean a job that didn't bore me, pay me next to nothing, or make me feel sub-human. I wanted something different, maybe even unusual, but I didn't know what that would be. Then fate deposited a grand opportunity at my feet.

I'd been looking for work in the small town of Prescott, Arizona, where my parents had relocated our family just six months earlier, but it wasn't panning out. Reluctantly, I expanded my quest to include Tucson, where a friend connected me with the U.S. Forest Service. The agency hired me as a timekeeper for an elite firefighting crew: The Catalina Hot Shots.

Thrilled, I couldn't imagine anything better than living and working in the pines of a National Forest. However, despite the fun as the only single woman among those strong, handsome young men, after two summers in that job, I realized that the Forest Service had far more interesting career options. Not only did I hate working indoors, I hated the tedious chore of filling out fifty timesheets a week, pressing my Number 2 pencil hard enough to imprint multiple carbon copies, forming blisters on my fingers. I applied for a more exciting job.

In 1976, at twenty-years-old, I became one of the first women hired as a wildland firefighter with the U.S. Forest Service. I had no fear of hard work and liked the idea of an outdoor job. Not for a moment did I think that this job was anything out of the ordinary for a woman. That I was the only female on the crew didn't faze me, either. This job felt like the perfect fit for me.

I never thought of myself as brave or strong. To me, brave and strong people are activists, astronauts, or doctors. I was just a young woman who wasn't afraid to take on the rigors of wildland firefighting. Tough, dangerous work? No problem. Lack of experience? I'd learn new things. Whether we were digging line on a wildfire dodging flames mere inches away, flying in helicopters, or performing routine maintenance of trails and campgrounds, I found the work both challenging and satisfying. I also discovered that pushing myself physically made me feel strong, invincible— both inside and out. What I hadn't anticipated was that men would resent my presence.

I'd only been on the job for a week when my crew had to dig a trench for a new waterline. As I swung a pick to loosen the rocky soil, one of my crewmates said, "I don't get why you'd want a job like this. Seems unlikely for a girl."

Annoyed, I asked, "So … what kind of job would you like me to have?"

The man scowled. "I like my women barefoot, pregnant, and in the kitchen."

Well, isn't that just great, I thought sarcastically.

Another crewmate didn't think I could load my fire gear into the back of our truck, despite the fact I'd been doing so for weeks. When I loaded my gear, he said snidely, "I guess I'm used to those helpless Southern Belles back home."

At the end of my first fire season, after battling a dozen fires, that same crewmate said, "You're just here to fulfill the Forest Service's woman minority quota. You make more work for everyone else! You should quit and go home."

All of these attempts to make me quit backfired. The harder these guys made it for me, the more I wanted that job. I learned how to deal with chauvinists that summer, and the next. But by my third fire season, the discrimination became formalized.

When a rainy summer ended my position early, I applied for a transfer. The firefighting position was given to one of the guys— one with less experience than me. Believing this to be a mistake, I met with the supervisor and asked why.

The man looked at me squarely and said, "Because I don't hire women on my fire crews."

Both he and I knew he couldn't legally do that, but at that moment, I let it go.

Later, I filed an Equal Employment Opportunity complaint. That went nowhere. It was his word against mine. That complaint would follow me into my fourth fire season, where I learned I'd been blacklisted.

Okay, those were the bad times. But there were plenty of good times. There were the men who supported and encouraged me. There was camaraderie unlike anything I'd ever experienced. We shared danger and excitement. We had fun! The pride I felt in my dangerous but fulfilling job was something I would never let anyone take from me. I continued as a firefighter for seven years.

But then the worst thing happened.

All of that hard work had destroyed both of my knees.

After multiple surgeries, which resulted in unrelenting pain and limited mobility, my doctor told me I would never be able to work on a fire crew again. Severely depressed, I believed my life was over. I contemplated suicide.

My counselor suggested a career test. This made me furious. I didn't want a new career. I wanted my old one back.

I yelled at him: "But I'll be thirty-four by the time I graduate!"

"Yes," he said, "But you'll be thirty-four in four years whether you go to college or not."

I smiled wryly. I didn't believe a career test would change my mind, but I took that stupid test. What did the computer place at the top of the list? Garbage collector! I almost ripped the test to shreds. The third option made me pause—I could be a landscape architect. I'd always loved plants, and I could use my creative side. The second option was similar, and it didn't require a degree. Although I'd never considered college, now I wanted to go more than anything—which is how I ended up graduating *summa cum laude* with a degree in landscape architecture.

That degree was just the first step. It took four years to acquire the work experience necessary to take the state exams for the title of Landscape Architect. While working for a civil engineering company in the booming land development business, I studied hard and passed those state exams. Many of my job tasks were helping people comply with legal landscape codes, but I also designed parks, streetscapes, and even a public educational garden. I enjoyed my new field. In addition, I earned enough income that I could end my unhappy marriage and start life over.

In 2008, shortly after divorcing and purchasing a home, my company laid me off. An economically tough time for me, and many others. Unemployment benefits ran out two years later, yet the economy had not improved. No company was hiring in my field. Terrified that I would lose my home, one day, sitting on the couch feeling despondent, I asked myself: What else can I do to earn a living using my education and experience?

An organization in my community offered adult education classes for residents. Perhaps if I can't practice what I know, I can teach it. I contacted them and pitched a class about desert landscaping. They said yes. I set the fee, of which they would take thirty percent for my use of their facilities. Sounded fair to me.

That class filled up, as did many of my subsequent classes.

It's been twelve years since I started teaching, and eleven years since I incorporated my landscape design business, fueled by students requesting my services.

Who knew I would end up loving to teach? Who knew that making a living on my own terms would be so satisfying? I didn't become rich, but I paid off my mortgage, and I can cover my bills. My wealth comes from the pride I feel when my students tell me how much they love my class. There's a bonus, too. Aside from sharing my expertise, I can incorporate my values into my teaching—something that would never fly in the corporate world. I stress water conservation, and why using native and drought-tolerant plants makes the most sense.

The resiliency I don't give myself credit for got me through some tough times—and no doubt I will need it in the future. Where does this resiliency come from? For me, it is being willing to look for alternatives to difficult situations, alternatives that fit my own terms, terms I can live with. This approach helps me move forward, even when, at first, I don't want to. I believe this is how I've survived tough setbacks that many people might not have.

Are you resilient? My guess is you are. You just haven't found a way to tap into it—yet.

***

Linda Strader became one of the first women hired on a U.S. Forest Service fire crew in Southern Arizona in 1976. She holds two degrees, and is a landscape architect, certified arborist, watercolor artist, and published author. Her work includes *Summers of Fire: A Memoir of Adventure, Love and Courage* published in May 2018, (Bedazzled Ink Publishing) and *Uprooted: A New Life in the Arizona Sun*, the prequel to *Summers of Fire*, published December 2021 (Bedazzled Ink Publishing).

13 | Speaking of Myself by P.A. O'Neil

I am a storyteller, not a liar, but a teller of tales. I have what's referred to as "The Gift of Gab." I will talk to anyone about anything. There have been times when talking has set me aside, for example, when I spent all of kindergarten and half of the Sixth Grade in the corner. The teachers punished me for speaking in class, but my parents never chided or punished me for talking. They reminded me to respect the rules of my teachers for speaking out of turn, but they always encouraged me to talk. Not that I had anything worthy to say, but because I actually could talk. There was a time when they thought I might forever be mute.

It was the middle of the last century when families lived in the suburbs and parents commuted to work. Children were left in the care of neighbors or with family members. Mama was a secretary, and every morning after breakfast, she would pack us up, kiss everyone goodbye, and head out to work. Daddy put me in the back seat with a small bag of clothes and food, then placed my infant sister in the bassinet on the floor behind the passenger seat. We'd drive to Nana and Tata's house, which was only a small detour from the route Daddy took to work, where he would drop us off with a kiss and a thank you to them. Then we'd settle down to our second breakfast.

Nana and Tata were in their sixties. They had raised five children, buried one, and after having lived through two world wars and a depression, were considered elderly by the standards of the day. Their youngest child was still at home finishing high school. He would be gone to school by the time we got there, but when he returned each afternoon, he'd grab a snack and lock himself in his bedroom. There he would do homework uninterrupted by an annoying toddler and a newborn.

I was the toddler, two-years old and not exactly verbal, but with enough words to get my point across.

Tata had been a machinist and had a shop in the garage, a place we were forbidden to enter for years. He spent most of his days there, coming in only for lunch to eat off a TV tray in the front room while he watched the news. He always drank his milk with ice cubes out of a Mason jar.

Every day the routine was the same, my sister was bathed and placed in her crib. She couldn't sit up yet, so her entertainment comprised the sunbeams floating over her bed from the open window. On that day, I heard her cooing and giggling to herself, and I wanted to know what she was doing.

Daringly, I placed the toe of my leather shoes on the decorative molding along the footboard of her crib. Stretching as far as my little arm would go, I caught hold of the top of the board, and, using all my strength, managed to grab it with my other hand as well. Stepping with my remaining foot I caught a toe-hold, or so I thought, as I peered over the edge of the crib to watch my sister wave her hands and babble as she swatted away the light.

Perched on my tiptoes, I stretched my head completely over the edge of the wooden crib until my feet slipped. My chin hit the top of the footboard, teeth bearing full force onto my tongue, nearly severing it but a thread. The pain was excruciating.

There are few things in this world you will never forget. This was one. Even though I was only two years old, I will never forget the pain of biting off my tongue.

I howled as tears flowed down my cheeks. I could not talk.

The baby screamed, which brought Nana from the next room to check her for a poking diaper pin. She didn't notice me right away because I had fallen mostly under the crib. As I emerged with a face full of tears, blood ran down my shirt. She put the screaming infant back in the bed and grabbed a cloth diaper, applying it to my mouth.

Scooping me up with one arm, the other pressed to my face, she ran to the back door. "Bill, Bill ..." she cried. "Help me, Sugar's been hurt!"

Tata lumbered out of the garage and into the house, wiping his hands on the rag he kept in the back pocket of his overalls. He found Nana at the sink, chilly water running from the tap, trying to rinse the now red cotton cloth. I sat on the drainboard, still in hysterics.

He looked at me and then at Nana. "What's this? Let me see, what did she do?"

"I don't know. She was back behind the end of the crib, the baby was crying, and I found her like this."

Tata placed one hand behind my head to hold it still while he pinched my cheeks with his grease-stained fingers, telling me to open my mouth. "My God, she's bitten her tongue off!"

***

If this had happened today, they would have rushed me to a hospital emergency room. But in those days, emergency rooms were for car crash victims, heart attacks, and women in labor. My grandparents took me to a local clinic specializing in Family Practice. Somewhere along the line, Tata ran to the neighbor's house asking if they would care for the baby. Armed with a bag full of cloths, he placed Nana and me in the back seat of the Jeep and drove away.

He asked, "Did you call her mother to meet us?"

"No, I couldn't take my hands away except to leave milk and diapers for the baby. I didn't want her to swallow it. We'll call her from the clinic," Nana responded.

Southern California in 1960 was a peaceful time. Suburbs were connected by larger streets and arterials, where businesses congregated. The community clinic was on one of these streets. The large waiting room was like those of today, with matching chairs grouped here and there offering a modicum of privacy. There were two doors, one off the street, the other into the exam rooms. A sliding window separated the reception desk from the crying babies, coughing children, and tired parents, all waiting their turn to see the doctor.

Tata parked and ran around the Jeep to let Nana out. He picked me up and followed her along the sidewalk to the door, all the while calmly telling me it would be all right. I had buried my head on his shoulder, still sobbing.

Once inside, Nana pushed aside a woman at the counter and demanded we immediately see the doctor.

"Hey, now, you can't ..." the other patient said gruffly to Nana. "Now, ma'am, I'm sure if you'll just sit down and wait your turn ..." the annoyed receptionist admonished.

"You don't understand. My granddaughter has bitten her tongue off."

The patient who had been pushed aside gasped as Tata walked up, my blood on the rags and his chest.

The receptionist called for a passing nurse, who, after a brief explanation, moved quickly to lead us toward an examination room.

***

Certain memories linger forever. This next is one of those memories. Though brief, it is as real as if it happened yesterday.

They immediately ushered us into a small room with a long examination table and a couple of chairs. They placed me on the table, a strap of leather pulled tight against my mid-section. Tata stood to the side with his hand on my chest as if imparting his strength into my small, frightened body. At first the nurse and then the doctor pulled open my mouth to assess how grievous the injury was. The doctor barked instructions and as the nurse set out his equipment. He called out to unseen others in the hallway.

When he returned, two more women, another clinic nurse, and the bookkeeper from the back office followed him. The three women, along with Nana, held down my limbs to keep from flailing.

Tata's hands embraced my head. Making a vice with his strong hands, he held my head still, my soft curls escaping through his fingers. With a practiced calm, the doctor used his thumb and forefinger to pull my tongue out as far as possible, carefully resting the dangling piece on his other fingers.

I remember wanting to fight, blinded by the overhead light and my own tears. Someone kept telling me to hold still. Through my wailing, I begged for Mama and for them to let me go with garbled noises because I couldn't talk. All the while, the physician was doing his best to stitch my tongue together.

This is where the memory fades, and probably for good reason.

The receptionist had called Mama, who flew from her work to the clinic. The doctor had insisted we stay after the procedure in case shock set in. The bleeding stopped, but the crying continued, this time sounding normal, my few words more developed. Nana said I had calmed enough for occasional moping gasps until Mama showed up, which is when a new batch of tears erupted.

The doctor warned we needed to watch for bleeding and infection. "The tongue is a resilient organ and will attempt to heal itself, but the graft might not take, which would mean further surgery and losing normal speech."

We all left the clinic with a sense of relief, but my parents and grandparents were cautious over the next few days, until the follow-up visit when the doctor proclaimed the entire tongue pink and healthy, with no need for further surgery.

Time progressed with no residual difficulty with my verbal development. My language skills progressed along with the decline of my curiosity about what my sister was doing. If Nana ever felt remorse over the incident, it wasn't for long. Nana was a wise woman. She understood you can't be everywhere, or hover over your children, and even if you did, unpleasant things could still happen.

Does speaking properly have anything to do with my ability to tell a good tale? I wouldn't know, but I can attest that the fact I can talk has taken me to many places to meet many people. Today I mostly talk through my keyboard, but if we ever met in person, I would offer you a cuppa and sit down to tell you a tale.

***

P.A. O'Neil's stories have been featured in over forty anthologies, on-line journals, and magazines. She and her husband reside in Thurston County, Washington. Four collections of her stories, *Witness Testimony and Other Tales* as well as *Two Sides of the Same Coin: In-between stories of Sherlock Holmes and John H. Watson*, are available on Amazon. For links to books which feature her stories, please visit her Amazon author page: P.A. O'Neil.

14 | Alone in Rome by Wendy Banks

It was 1968 and friends suggested we leave the grey clouds of England and go to Sardinia for a summer of sunshine and fun. We were cocky twenty-year-olds doing our best to look like Twiggy, striding around London in our mini-skirts and uncomfortable platform boots. We quit our dull office jobs and took off. Swimming in the warm, turquoise Mediterranean, feeling the sand, the sea breeze, such freedom! We flirted with the handsome Italians swarming around us in the cafes of Alghero and almost immediately I was madly in love with one irresistibly handsome boy with wavy black hair and deep eyes.

Most people don't take their vacation romance home with them, but I did. Franco was eager to learn English and get away from his over-protective mother. We "nested" in a small studio flat in London on the top floor of a Victorian building. I got a secretarial job right away, but Franco didn't have a work visa. He needed a sponsor for that.

"I can't tell my mother I'm a dishwasher," he said.

We applied to Italian companies where he was sure a wonderful career would blossom. He got hired for various jobs, but they were short-lived. I was happy to play big mama and support him through these disappointments.

"I couldn't do this without you," he told me. "You're my rock, my lovely angel, and you always make me laugh!"

And laugh we did. We'd race up the long flight of stairs and tumble into our flat with a tickling fight. After all the fizzled job prospects, but now fluent in English, Franco returned to Italy. I intended to join him a few weeks later. For two weeks straight, I cried. It seemed so sudden, such a wrench. I missed his loving arms and sweetness.

As soon as I saw him at Rome airport, I had a sinking feeling it was over. I tried to ignore it at first. We stayed with his sister and her extended family, and I looked for work while he ran around with friends to escape his relatives' noisy scoldings and gesticulations that looked abusive. Our whole dynamic had changed. He didn't need me. After a couple of uncomfortable weeks, with no English-speaking jobs on the horizon and my money running out, I was on the point of booking a flight home when his sister pointed to an ad, in Italian. It said "International company," and she insisted I call.

Trembling at the thought of having to speak more than "pronto" I called, and an English voice answered. I got the job. Miraculously, too, I found an apartment. But Franco still seemed like a different person. We just didn't fit anymore. I felt like an outsider, foreign to him and his family. Our chemistry had vanished. As I was no longer in love with him, I broke it off. I was alone and scared, but the discomfort of being in a dead relationship was worse. Despite his frequent visits and pleas, I held my ground. Somehow, I managed to go forward blindly, push through the fear, and stick with what, deep down, felt right.

The clerical job was tedious, collating sales figures and hand-drawing endless graphs that challenged my poor mathematical ability, but I sunk my teeth into it. After all, I was in Rome! I could walk to work, pop into a café for an espresso and a pastry on my way to work, which was so Italian. I'd stop in the little piazzas and watch the sunlight sparkle in the fine spray of the fountains, listen to Italian voices as neighbors called to each other from their roof gardens and across balconies festooned with flowers. Even the birds seemed to sing in Italian. I smiled at how lucky I felt to be in this magical city and not in foggy, grey London. At work, my boss was delightful, and co-workers were pleasant, although none became friends. My rent was high, so I couldn't afford a phone, making me feel doubly isolated.

I really missed the love and companionship I'd had with Franco in London. After work, I'd walk home to my empty apartment with its cold tiled floor, a dark basement on a busy street. I'd fry an egg, study Italian, and try to tune out the traffic noise. One day, tired of watching people's feet walk by, I took a bus, just to see a bit more of the city. I stood pressed in and jostled on the crowded bus, surrounded by people, not understanding anything they were saying. Then I felt something on my thigh, my hip, and then slide onto my behind.

"Eh! Scusi!" I said loudly.

I turned around but couldn't see whose slimy hand had so rudely insulted me. How dare he violate me like that! I pushed through to the door and got off at the next stop. I wasn't even wearing a mini-skirt. Sadly, foreign women were considered fair game, and I often heard "puttana" muttered under the breath, which means prostitute.

As I walked home, I wondered if I should just leave and go home? To another boring job and dutiful weekend visits to my mother and listen to her whining? That situation had become so depressing, repellent even, it held no allure for me. All through my teens, I'd tried to fix her marriage and now she was divorced and still unhappy.

"Hi Mom, how are you?"

"Oh, alright I suppose. My arthritis is acting up again, and it's been raining for weeks on end."

"Oh, I'm sorry. Are you taking the meds I got for you from the doctor?" I'd wait for the next complaint.

"Oh dear, I think the house is just too big for me. It's such a lot of work."

"But Mum, you love your cottage, the garden, the village! Does something need fixing?"

"Oh the garden, it's too much for me to handle."

At least she wasn't berating my father. I told myself not to expect any questions about how I was or what I was doing.

It was dark when I finally got home. I trudged up to my door and as I turned on the light, huge black, beetle-like creatures scuttled into corners. At least three inches long, I'd never seen such large bugs before. I ran up to the portiere—the apartment manager. He was in his fifties, sullen, with a pale, pudgy face and greasy hair.

I tried to tell him in my limited Italian, "There are many things … how do you say … big, black, with legs," miming legs and feelers and my angst.

As always, he was uninterested but reluctantly came down to see. Of course, there was no sign of the critters.

He just shrugged and said, "Fa caldo," which means it's hot. Like, what did I expect!

"Yes, but I saw them. They were right there!"

He didn't care. What was I doing here? I began missing Franco and started to wish he was here by my side, and we were living together.

I kept the light on in the hallway, hoped they wouldn't come out and went to bed. With the oppressiveness in the apartment, I opened the horizontal wooden slats of the window blind a couple of inches to let in some air, even though it was dusty, because my window sat level with the sidewalk. I shed a few tears and went to sleep.

In the middle of the night, I heard a tap, tap, tap at my window. A man was crouched at the open window, moving the slats up one by one, making a space at the bottom to put a hand through and push the window up. For a moment, I was frozen. Then he shined a flashlight at me.

I jumped out of bed, ran to the window yelling, "Get out of here! Vai, vai! Mannaggia la miseria!"

I grabbed the cord of the blind, yanked it down with a bang. He slunk off.

Shaking, I locked all the windows and doors. Trying to comfort myself, I made some hot milk, spilling most of it. What to do? I had no phone. I wasn't going outside. So I went back to bed. But I couldn't sleep. Every few minutes, I looked at the window, re-checking it. But still I couldn't sleep, so I dragged my bed into the hallway, shut the bedroom door and put a chair up against the door handle. I left the light on hoping to keep the bugs away. I put a scarf around my eyes to keep out the light.

Next day I dragged myself to work. I just couldn't bring myself to tell my co-workers or my boss about it. What could they do anyway? I couldn't face the drama, people feeling sorry for me and offering me a place to stay. Just too embarrassing. I was raised the British way never to make a fuss. And call the polizia? I didn't have a description of the man. What could they do? I imagined them sneering at me, a single girl living alone … "puttana."

After work I went to the portiere to ask for his help. I explained as best I could in my terrible Italian, with a lot of gestures.

For once, he seemed interested. He asked, "Lo avete visto?" "Huh?" Visto, la faccia?" he pointed to his eyes, his face.

"No, I didn't see his face. Polizia?" I asked.

He shrugged, "Beh …! Shook his head, "E Agosto," he said, it's August, "Fa caldo, sirocco …" It's hot, the sirocco winds from Africa.

Oh great. So this was a normal thing. I went into my apartment, boiled some spaghetti and watched for bugs. There was something "off" about this guy. Then it dawned on me. It's him! I think it's him! Tomorrow I planned to look him in the eye and tell him I've remembered his face and would go to the police.

For months, I slept in the hallway and kept the windows bolted shut. I also bought a fan so I wouldn't completely suffocate. I was lonesome and scared. I wondered if I should just give up. I remembered my father referring to the Blitz, saying that the British just had to keep calm and carry on. He said they were willing to "fight them on the beaches" and that if ever you felt down, think of Churchill, pull your socks up and keep on.

I had slowly learned to be self-reliant and strong. As soon as I had enough money, I bought a moped, which gave me more freedom to tool around Rome and avoid the buses. I took art history and Italian classes, made friends. One friend, Sheila, became my roommate. She had a gorgeous Italian boyfriend who had an equally gorgeous friend. I fell in love with him. We made a great foursome. Our boyfriends wined and dined us and took us out to countless amazing restaurants in this magical city, day trips to the Abruzzi Mountains, weekend jaunts to Naples, Orvieto.

By six months, I'd learned to speak enough Italian to get by and had created a fulfilling life filled with new friends and a passion for the art history in Rome. Antonio was twelve years older than me. He already had a career as a doctor and didn't want me to help him learn English. Sheila married Mario, but Antonio didn't propose, and I probably wouldn't have said yes. Perhaps it didn't feel right because he didn't seem to need me. Two years later, circumstances took me back to England. At that time, I wanted to do something with my life beyond marrying and being a housewife. With my newfound strength and confidence, I wanted a career. Another ex-pat girlfriend told me how I could go to college and get a teaching credential or even a degree in education. I applied.

It wasn't easy going back to London. It was like starting all over again. Finding a flat to share was arduous, and the first one I got was miserable. I didn't know if my application would be accepted. The temporary jobs were mind-numbing and tearful phone calls to Antonio tore me up. But I'd followed my heart in Rome, learned not to depend on anyone and push through the fear and loneliness toward the right path for me. Whenever I felt low, I'd remind myself I wasn't dealing with huge bugs or a peeping tom, and I didn't need to worry about feeling lonesome. It would not last forever. I could tap my strength, not settle, and keep moving forward. My experience in Rome had forever changed me.

I was accepted into the teaching college, and it gave me a wonderful education. Having developed independence and self-confidence, I was able to love and support my mother without feeling emotionally drained. I'd learned to trust my feelings in future life-changing decisions. A few years later, I had the courage to leave a relationship that was going nowhere and do what felt right, however painful. I left, seizing an opportunity to come to the U.S. It was the best decision I ever made!

***

Wendy Banks grew up in the lush countryside of Sussex in the U.K. She went to drama school, traveled, helped a renowned potter write a book and worked as a script supervisor in films. She was the Astrological Editor for a publisher in L.A. and studied writing with Jack Grapes. She loves storytelling, volunteering abroad, teaching yoga in a prison, dancing, and playing with her grandsons.

15 | Point of Pivot by Avesha Michael

I was sitting in my car frozen in fear. Reluctantly, I got out and went into the urgent care. I felt overwhelmed with shame and was focused on how I could explain this away, yet still get the care I needed.

My biggest fear was that the man I was involved with, whose business was down the street, would be contacted if the truth came out. I was more concerned about protecting him than the painful and injured state of my wrist.

This wasn't just my left wrist and hand; this was my livelihood. Pottery was my craft and full-time business, my greatest love since I was a little girl growing up in Chicago. And this injury had occurred less than a year after risking it all to open my first pottery studio in Los Angeles. This was the beginning of my very first busy season, the holidays, when I made most of my annual income.

In the waiting room, I sat in searing pain for what felt like hours. Then finally, the doctor called me in. The elderly physician reminded me of my grandpa, with the same salt and pepper hair and bushy eyebrows. He looked at my wrist and then asked the question I most dreaded.

"What happened?" He said as he touched my wrist. I winced in pain.

I felt my stomach tighten, my chest constricted. "I do pottery full time and I injured my wrist over-extending on the wheel," I explained.

The truth was far more horrifying; I had been violently assaulted. The night before, the man I was dating, bent back my wrist in anger and nearly broke it. It happened down the same street at a hole in the wall bar. It was the shittiest dive bar in Venice.

This man I was seeing frequented this place often, due to the good "tap" beer. It had an old wooden bar that wrapped the entire room. Loud TVs blared sports in every corner.

We were standing at the bar when it happened in slow motion. He became angry and violently folded back my left hand. In a blink I succumbed, as I found myself slowly crouching to the floor to minimize the pain. Sliding down against the bar, I thought my hand was going to snap, my throwing wrist.

I sank to the floor, pleading for him to stop, with tears streaming. I was utterly helpless. As I crouched shriveled on the filthy floor, the sweet, stunning Native American bartender came running around to me, gasping, "Are you okay? "Are you okay?" In shock and seething pain, I simply nodded, shrouded in despair.

Driving home, I felt heartbroken and in complete shock. Even after this violent assault, I didn't want him to leave me there alone. Being left by him hurt more than my injured wrist. The trigger of my abandonment wound came out in full force.

These haunting moments came flashing back, as the doctor took X-rays, manipulated my hand and concluded it wasn't broken, just badly injured. I wish I could say it was a relief, but it wasn't. Without my hand, there would be no mugs, no bowls, and no income. But, even worse, I would let all my buyers down in stores across the country.

The doctor tried to comfort the tears I was clearly holding back and said, "Don't worry, you'll heal and will be okay."

But I barely heard him, and I surely didn't believe him. I felt my work and my life were ruined.

Then he landed the gut-wrenching news. "I'm sorry to say this, but you won't be throwing pottery anytime soon."

My jaw dropped open in devastation. He injected me with cortisone to help with the acute pain and gave me a brace that went halfway up my arm.

"Remember, don't use your hand for anything. Give it a chance to heal," he said as he left the exam room.

I paid my bill and left.

As I went back to my car and started the engine, I burst into tears. My head fell forward into the steering wheel, and I wept, feeling completely hopeless. I sat in the parking lot staring into the cinderblock wall in front of me, unable to fathom how I would manage this injury. I was on the brink of losing my lifelong dream. As the tears streamed down my face, I knew I had to do the one thing I dreaded the most: ask for help. Having grown up in poverty and a life of struggle, I resolved to be self-sufficient, and not depend on others. However, I remembered a Facebook group for women, Inspired Women of Los Angeles. These women showed up in remarkable ways for each other, offering jobs, internships, and sharing wins while supporting one another.

I got to my studio and sat at my desk, next to my pottery wheel, and wrapped my right hand around my left wrist, just holding it tenderly as if it was an injured baby bird wing. Then I posted a need for interns on this Facebook group page. I offered to teach them in exchange for helping me on the hand-building end, in creating vessels I would be selling all holiday season. It could turn it into a win-win.

This was my point of pivot. Instead of quitting, I would do what it took to preserve my livelihood and my beloved business. I would not let ten seconds of violence take away the lifelong dream I had just begun.

I changed my technique from wheel throwing on a pottery wheel to slab work, in which clay is rolled into flat pieces and formed into functional wares. It's a different process and aesthetic. I had major shows and craft fairs in a few weeks, and several stores were counting on me for their holiday season. The pressure was mountainous and the overwhelming stress unbearable.

I was floored when dozens of women answered my Facebook post, and several female interns came to work with me in my studio in Culver City. They helped me create an entirely new line, with all new designs.

There was Kim, the dominatrix, who created videos with her partner and worked in a dungeon by LAX. She would often bring her cat to my studio and sit the carrier on my kiln while we worked. There was Brea, the yoga teacher, who brought her dog to the studio regularly. She met her husband overseas and found healthy love after escaping her own abusive relationship of many years. There was Nellie, who desperately needed work and ended up becoming my assistant for the next four years. On the first day, she shared that she dealt with manic depression and excessive drinking. Her brash authenticity was such a relief.

While they rolled out slabs of clay with a rolling pin and made cylinders into planters, vases, and cups, my days shifted from working with clay, to providing oversight. All the while, I held my shameful secret of what really happened from my interns, my mom, and my friends. They didn't know he had physically injured me. And they didn't know I was still seeing him.

Sadly, I stayed with him for years, until we went into lockdown at the beginning of the pandemic. That forced a separation. His physical abuse had only escalated, so this separation felt like a divine intervention. What I learned from a trauma therapist later was that I had lived with CPTSD (Complex Post Traumatic Stress Disorder), due to complex trauma occurring throughout my entire life. I experienced prolonged and acute trauma starting at birth, which led me repeatedly into toxic relationships. My current relationship was not the first one where I experienced domestic violence. These relationships reflected my view of my own self-worth. Living with complex trauma leads to intense self-blame, which only fuels the unhealthy relationship dynamic. I became isolated from most of my close family and friends and trauma bonded with this man. I felt undeserving of anything else and desperate for love, which was never attainable. The cycle was vicious and demoralizing. The immense shame kept me silent and took me years to unravel and heal in therapy.

Despite all this, and during this crisis, I designed pieces that ended up being best sellers. I used 22K gold to write inspirational words on mugs, a beautiful extension of support to others. To hold a warm mug in your hands and start your day with gratitude, love, and the reminder to "dream big" was a sweet gift to give. I couldn't keep these designs on my studio shelves for years to come. I shipped them around the world for nearly a decade.

As a result of my reaching out for help when I needed it, I discovered my own real strength. I realized that connection and community are truly everything. I began to recognize my ability to problem solve and how well I could resource myself.

Through this experience, the greatest healing is the journey I took inside myself. I found tools that supported me tremendously. After waiting nearly a year for therapy, I was finally paired with an incredible trauma therapist at The Relational Center, an essential non-profit that became my lifeline. Kristina helped me save my own life. She became the first secure attachment I ever experienced, and through this safety and unconditional support, I gradually exited from this abusive relationship. This process, more than anything, created the foundation of showing up for myself in a new way. I started seeking out additional trauma healing and through her nudging, ended up joining an underground Domestic Violence support group.

The other essential part of my healing was in discovering breathwork, which I felt the universe led me to find. After a lifetime of exploring many healing modalities, this was the greatest embodiment tool I had ever come across. If there's one thing domestic violence and shock trauma does, it dissociates and disembodies you from your own body. This tool helped me come back into my own body and feel it fully. As I became more embodied, I created a sense of safety within myself for the first time in my life. Nothing changed overnight, it was a daily practice of learning to listen to my own feelings, honoring them, and nurturing the sensitivity in me after a lifetime of abandoning them. I also discovered sound healing, inner child work, and shadow work, all of which helped me come home to myself and create safety and trust from within. I became a breath-work facilitator, trained Reiki Master and now use writing and storytelling as an integral part of my ongoing healing and in supporting myself and others.

While this experience was horrifying, I chose to get support and saved my own life. I finally chose myself by consciously attending to my pain while honoring my deepest needs. Transmuting the trauma into healing is an ongoing journey. And now that I've broken the cycle, I can extend my support to others from a place of deep empathy.

***

Avesha Michael is a ceramic artist, writer, storyteller, and photographer. She holds an MA in Spiritual Psychology, is a Breathwork Teacher, Reiki Master and is in training for Integrative Somatic Trauma Therapy. Avesha is deeply committed to speaking truth to story, bringing awareness to mental health and trauma-informed shared human experiences. She believes connection is everything. She wants chickens and goats one day and is counting the days until she can escape the city and start a peaceful homestead.

16 | Oh, Five Is Such a Pretty Number! by Elizabeth Smiley

I'd ticked-off all the prerequisite boxes before having a baby: college, law school, passing the bar, and a walk down the aisle. I wanted a big family: five kids. For a year, my husband and I tried, but a baby-bump didn't manifest. So I sought counsel from my ob-gyn. My history of irregular cycles, I learned, meant I wasn't ovulating. After years of taking precautions sans abstinence to avoid conception and hair pulling when my cycles were confused with being late, I couldn't get pregnant. THWACK! Smacked upside the head by Mother Nature. Conceiving was not going to be easy-peasy.

My ob-gyn prescribed Clomid, a mild ovulation kick-starter. I still hoped to conceive on my own and I was deterred by Clomid's side effects, like multiple births.

"You aren't taking the Clomid?" My doctor asked incredulously. She wasted no time delving into my hesitation and ordered a diagnostic procedure to detect blockage in my fallopian tubes that might hinder an egg from descending. "It gets the gunk out and gets everything flowing."

To avoid agitating my doctor, I abided by her orders and took a sick day from my job as lead chair in an Abuse and Neglect courtroom of Juvenile Court to lie on a table in a windowless, gray room in the sub-basement of the hospital. As my ob-gyn filled my uterine cavity with blue dye and was about to flip a switch to zap an image of my insides, I tried not to think about my friend's caution, "That procedure could blow out your tubes."

I considered bailing. I fantasized about scooping up and fleeing with one of those kids who passed through my courtroom. It was possible without security cameras. No one would notice me walking

99

out the door with a child, and it was probable no one would report the child kidnapped. Ultimately, I resisted these temptations.

Fortunately, there was no blockage and my tubes remained intact. However, I needed a fertility specialist. I climbed onto a merry-go-round where things were done to me, and I spun on autopilot.

During this time, I was promoted to Felony Review, a position that required me to approve felony charges for freshly arrested suspects and wrangle signed confessions, which at times, took thirty-six hours.

In a groggy stupor, I submitted to rounds of blood draws administered by phlebotomists not always skilled with deep vein pokes and I received daily injections of Pergonal, a follicle-stimulating hormone harvested from menopausal nuns' pee. Yes, their holy waters contained otherwise forsaken hormones and the genesis of "be fruitful and multiply." Pergonal also had side effects, like Ovarian Stimulation Syndrome. Extra hormones could cause blood clots in my legs and cause the blood vessels in my ovaries to leak gallons of fluid into my abdominal cavity. It was worth it to hold a baby in my arms.

For months I peed on a white stick and averted cradling the stick while I waited, valiantly following the instructions not to peek at the developing results for those interminable three minutes.

Then I parted ways with my office. The following month, I saw the coveted double blue lines! I'd crossed the finish line and become a member of the Expecting Mommy Club. I was giddy as I purchased the newbie pregnancy handbook: *What to Expect When You're Expecting* and immediately started wearing maternity clothes.

A whiff of my perfume, Clinique Happy, or garlic made me queasy, and chocolate tasted like plastic. I zestfully nibbled saltine crackers and bid adieu to perfume and garlic, but chocolate? Yes! A paltry cross to bear.

Just before Christmas, my husband and I departed to Florida. I packed my new red maternity bathing suit. Throughout our trip, I trickled. I presumed I was incontinent, a side-effect of pregnancy, and made a note to master Kegels.

Once back home, I went for my twenty-week ultrasound. Store windows were festooned with holiday cheer. But not for me. After a few swipes of the ultrasound wand across my abdomen, the tech excused herself to fetch the doctor.

My doctor delivered the news soberly. "You've lost a sink full of amniotic fluid … The baby can't move … The baby's limbs can't develop … Possibly an infection … Sorry."

My ears took in bits and pieces. The merry-go-round stopped. I recalled a girl I knew in college whose birth control was wearing red to conjure the Period Goddess after unprotected sex. She'd been reckless. I'd been flippant. Getting pregnant wasn't the end, it was only the beginning. No more baby because of that damn red bathing suit.

The doctor inserted Laminaria, a seaweed that would dilate my cervix. The next day I would be submitting to a curettage, a surgical procedure to scrape out my womb, which could potentially perforate my uterus and leave scar tissue.

That night, I was in pain. Little did I know I was having contractions. As my husband and I raced to the hospital, I grunted at him, "Run the red lights."

At the hospital, I asked everyone if I was in labor. No one answered as they ran around frantically. It turns out I was.

Afterward, I consoled myself. Giving birth was better. A nurse handed me a card with my baby's tiny, inked footprints. As I held my baby, my mind rejected the harsh reality of my dead dream and concentrated on forming a lasting picture of her.

After a blur of days, I bought a wooden box with a glass top and tenderly filled it with mementos: the white stick with the double blue lines, the pregnancy calendar, the cards that shouted

"Congratulations!" and the tiny footprints belonging to legs that would never walk. Then I walked on the beach along Lake Michigan, cried, and said goodbye.

I felt rudderless. My identity had switched from brash prosecutor to gentle mother to empty vessel. I refused to surrender to my body's failures and to return to my old life. Instead, I succumbed again to the merry-go-round. Back to the needle pokes, injections, and ultrasounds. Back to the parade of negative pregnancy tests. Months passed. I believed in my body's ability to get pregnant. It had happened before; it would happen again.

The following summer, my husband and I were in Atlanta for the Olympics when I got my period. Timing was everything, and the clock was ticking. To make the 7 a.m. appointment at the fertility office in Chicago the next morning, we'd have to drive through the night or wait another month. He wasn't waiting. We pulled into the driveway at 5 a.m. in time for a catnap and then another round of needles.

Daily Pergonal injections had to be administered at the same time, no exceptions, even in the middle of the "I do's" at a friend's wedding. As my husband and I commandeered a unisex bathroom we were interrupted by a fellow guest, who had begun celebrating early, banging on the door, "You gonna be in there longer?"

Using a syringe, I hastily withdrew from a vial the elixir that would coax at least one of my eggs to ripen and then I handed it to my husband. He fumbled. Over more banging, he jabbed the syringe into my backside. Blood bubbled up. He dabbed me with toilet paper, and I collected the drug paraphernalia.

As we exited, we were accosted by the door-banging guest. "I know what you were up to." He winked as he swirled his drink.

A few days later, my doctor found ripe eggs. And a few days after that, my husband and I returned to the doctor's office for my insemination. My husband's role: deliver a viable sample of his genetic material. My role: lie back and relax. During my insemination I thought of the other wannabe parents in the waiting room and mused, if there's a mix-up and I'm inseminated with some other hopeful dad's material, who will my baby resemble? My husband and I weren't supposed to have sex post-insemination, but for added measure, we did.

Then just like the previous year, a white stick revealed double blue lines. I danced. Pregnant again!

Another week later, I dialed my husband's work number. After one ring, he picked up.

"There's two." I announced, clutching the ultrasound picture marked "Twin A" and "Twin B."

Thereafter, the fertility treatment merry-go-round was replaced with a perilous pregnancy roller coaster. My twin pregnancy had the same due date as my last: May first. Each milestone, hearing heart beats for the first time, feeling first kicks, led to a jumble of elation and foreboding.

When I began spotting blood, we went to the hospital. When I passed a blood clot, a squishy black mass, we went to the hospital. After each scare, the doctors deemed us stable. But as a precaution, they put me on bed rest. My doctors wanted me in the hospital, but we seized a condo nearby. They granted me a reprieve but warned: three strikes and you're out. Additional mishaps meant hospitalized bed rest for my pregnancy's duration.

I learned that twins are typically born prematurely. My doctor prescribed steroids to develop the babies' lungs. More shots. Then I learned I had placenta previa. My pregnancy had implanted low in my womb, which meant I was carrying a high-risk pregnancy. The placenta could rupture and all of us could die. My doctor bluntly told me there would be no travel. "You could bleed-out on the side of the highway."

But this time, I'd made it through Christmas.

My energies were mobilized into maintaining this pregnancy. While I laid on my left side, I devoured books about twins and picked out a layette. But nothing pink or blue, rather unisex yellow and green. It wasn't safe to be complacent with the looming threat of calamity.

At my seventh month, an ultrasound revealed more concerns: both babies were breech and were developing at different rates. News of a C-section caused me to squirm, but measurements indicating an eighteen percent differential caused me to quiver. The placenta wasn't nourishing both twins. Above a twenty percent differential doctors could intervene. One twin is terminated to save the other. I feared losing another baby, but remained serene to save at least one.

On March first, strike three occurred. I was leaking. My husband, who didn't own a cell phone, was running errands. I fought the urge to collapse onto myself and wrote, "went to the hospital" on a yellow Post-it Note and hailed a cab.

Within minutes after arriving at the hospital, I was having an emergency C-section two months before my due date. I was a mishmash of paralyzing inertia and acute attentiveness. I tried to glean clues from the medical professionals swirling about to assess whether my babies and I were going to make it out of this debacle alive.

I had the power to disassociate when I wasn't in charge. And I called on this power now. When Twin A kicked and ruptured the barrier between his inside water and his outside air environments. When a nurse weighed me, and I'd gained eighty pounds in seven months. When the resident anesthesiologist ordered a spinal. I questioned. An epidural was the birth plan. The resident vanished to fetch the Chief of Anesthesiology.

During the delay, my husband materialized.

The Chief administered the spinal, and my son was born through a horizontal incision of my womb. I held my breath, and my daughter was born. The twins weighed approximately three pounds, nine ounces and three pounds, eight ounces. The numbing trepidation of choosing to sacrifice one baby to save another had been unfounded. The next day I was wheeled into the Neonatal Intensive Care Unit (NICU) and held my two living, breathing babies against my chest to synchronize our heartbeats.

They were scrawny, but my heart was bursting. I wanted to shout like the Whos in Who-ville, "They are here!" But I was cautious. They hadn't developed the sucking reflex, so I fed them my pumped breast milk using a syringe and a tube that traveled from their noses into their stomachs. They also couldn't maintain their body temperature. I knew that babies with birthweights over two pounds survived, so I was optimistic.

After a month in the NICU, the babies were thriving. I exchanged their layette for pink and blue, bundled them up and brought them home. I had crossed the finish line. Finally, I relaxed and settled into being a new mom.

Four years later, we capitulated to the fertility doctor again. I was to return when I got my period, but my period didn't flow. It turned out I was already pregnant!

A few weeks later, my husband was out scrounging up Lays potato chips and Baskin-Robbins peanut butter chocolate ice cream for me. When he returned home, he found me in the bathroom. I'd miscarried. I wrapped the baby, placed her in a cooler, and we left for the hospital.

A resident inquired, "How do you know you were pregnant? Were there products of conception?" As if she were asking me at the grocery check-out, "Paper or plastic?"

The hospital lost the contents of the cooler. So no pathology report. I wanted to scream at the incompetence, but I kept my mouth shut because I needed a D & C. This time the procedure was completed, but I could get pregnant au naturel!

A few months later, I got pregnant again without doctors or needles. Another daughter, this time delivered without a C-section, weighing the combined birthweight of her siblings. I dry-coughed, peeing myself on the ride home. I couldn't have cared less. Three was my favorite number and now my family was complete.

***

Elizabeth Smiley is a "recovering lawyer" who spent most of her legal tenure as a prosecutor in Chicago's Juvenile Court. She is a mom of three—twins, plus one for fun, and a rescue puppy-dog. She was an Editorial Assistant and Contributor for *Quintessential New Trier Magazine*. Currently, she is revising her five picture books and researching a middle grade novel.

17 | Claiming My Name, Becoming the Storm by Raine Grayson

My family is fighting—but at least the meteorologist has forecasted rain.

I stand on my tippy-toes to reach the doorknob, using all the might my eight-year-old body can muster to swing the door open. I plop myself onto the cold linoleum and strain my neck to see outside, barely able to peek over the edge of the screen door. The storm hasn't started yet, but I can feel it beginning to brew. The air is thick and the world outside is dulled by an overcast of heavy clouds.

"You aren't even going to care when I die. When I die, you'll be dancing on my grave. It doesn't matter that I'm your mother, and that I raised you—you can't wait for me to die!" My grandmother screams to my mother in the next room over.

It's a fight I've heard a hundred times before. My father is out of the picture. I only have these two women, who hate each other, to look to as parental figures.

Sitting in front of the screen door is where I can always be found in times like these. The weather channel is a permanent fixture on the miniscule TV my family keeps in the kitchen. It's come to be my favorite channel. I am as familiar with the local weather forecasters as I am with Steve from *Blues Clues*, my other favorite thing to watch. I only turn it off when I know a storm is near.

"You raised me? Is that what you want to call it? You treated me like shit my whole life! You'll probably curse me with your dying breath!"

I watch as the rain falls, making peaceful patterns on my wooden deck, turning it dark in a speckling motion, like a Monet painting. I lose myself in the earthy, heavy smell and the persevering

107

wall of sound. The rain is a manifestation of serenity to me, something I desperately need as I try to survive in my turbulent and abusive household.

"Blame everything on me! While you're out drinking and doing Lord knows what else, I'm stuck back here, taking care of your rotten children!"

The silver serenade of the wind turns the leaves back like pages being flipped in a book the world can't wait to know the end of. In this moment of thunder-studded serenity, I feel like I'm in a painting. The world is fresh and beautiful in a way I thought could only exist in art.

I decide to name myself after the rain. It will be an act of claiming that beautiful peace for myself; a peace I'm desperate for as I listen to my family scream at each other from the other room. Some sounds can only truly be drowned out by a good storm.

I adopt the name Raine, adding an "e" at the end to differentiate myself from the weather. First, it starts as a nickname. I timidly try it out in the online chat rooms I sneak onto in the middle of the night. It immediately feels so right that I start to become uncomfortable using the name given to me by my parents. Slowly, I start introducing myself to new friends as Raine. Over the years, it catches on. By age thirteen, Raine has become my name, even if it isn't legally so on paper. I even convince my family to call me Raine.

The act of claiming my name instills in me the power of the storm. It's thanks to this power that I scramble my way out of my abusive household. At fifteen, my grandmother dies and my mother, an alcoholic unable to keep a steady enough job to continue paying our rent, starts squatting. The place that was once my childhood home becomes dark and lonely as all of the utilities slowly get turned off. When she's finally caught, she moves us into a ghetto. Her crack addiction gets worse. My younger sibling, twelve at the time, is urinated on as some sort of sick prank played by our upstairs neighbors. They are too young to fully comprehend the squalor and abuse we are experiencing, but I'm not. I can't live like this. I leave, choosing a life of couch hopping and homelessness over putting my future in my mother's incapable hands.

As I pack up to leave, I remind myself of the power of the storms I'm named after. If the rain can happen anywhere, then so can I. Weather is always on the move, right? If it weren't, then my friends, the forecasters, would be out of the job.

My high school years are tough. I graduate, albeit barely. I feel worn down and exhausted and am often the victim of relentless bullying. One thing, however, remains untouchable: my name.

Even though it's not what my legal IDs reflect, I always state on day one of class that I would like to be called Raine. It's a demand, not a request. It doesn't matter if a piece of paper or driver's license says otherwise; I am Raine. Even though I'm a profoundly anxious child, I assert the importance of my name with such confidence that no one questions it. In fact, it's immediately so clear that I must be called Raine that if a teacher or peer refuses to do so, it sets the entire room on edge.

Defying the rule of my name turns someone into a red flag—a display of how to not respect people's boundaries. Even amongst my bullies, no one dares call me anything but Raine. My name, more than anything else, is an undeniable truth about me.

That unwavering belief I have in my name eventually becomes a pathway to understanding I deserve respect, and by my late teens, I finally carve out a life for myself. I have a shoddy apartment, a full-time job, and I start college. Overwhelmed, with only myself to guide me through the trials of early adulthood, I start smoking cigarettes. It keeps me awake during my long drives over the mountaintops of the Hudson Valley I must take to get to my college campus from my overnight job. I go days without sleeping and push myself beyond exhaustion, desperate for something to give me the strength to keep my eyes open through it all. The drag of a cigarette makes my lungs feel the same way I felt when I was a child, breathing in the petrichor air on my kitchen floor. I cling to the addiction as a way to harness the stormy power I was worried I might forget I held.

When I'm about to graduate college, a friend tells me that people smoke cigarettes for the same reason white men golf—because they don't know how to get fresh air for themselves.

This statement resonates with me. I stop smoking and start sitting on my apartment stoop every time there's a rainstorm. I take a deep breath and am filled with the same sense of peace I experienced as a child. Things are different, though. Now, I'm starting to understand what peace can look like outside of a painting. My partner, who will one day become my spouse, also joins me in my ritual and shares in the peace with me.

Quitting smoking and returning to my childhood ritual reminds me that changing the status quo is possible. I am reminded that, much like the way my high school self so voraciously defended my name, when I believe I deserve something fervently enough, it becomes an unmovable truth. Any resistance to that truth simply sloughs off your life in a way so mundane, so unremarkable, that it cannot penetrate your sense of self.

Even now, when people challenge me, I refuse to let them belittle me.

At thirty-one, after I legally changed my name and had been living as Raine for two thirds of my life, an older gentleman accosts me about my identity. It happens while my spouse and I are on vacation. We both love to make new friends and we meet an older man and his wife. They are decked out in Hawaiian shirts and have the welcoming appearance of two folks who have happily settled into their retirement. We have a lovely chat over dinner about the drinks we planned to order the next day, and the two of them give us some tips on fun things to do in the area.

As many people do, however, the man shows his true colors in the early hours of the morning after a liberal amount of alcohol.

Without being invited, he sits down at our table while we are enjoying music at the bar. Our guard is down. We welcome him to our table.

"So, RACHEL ..." he blabbers, leaning out of his chair and smirking as he gets in my face, trying to prove he guessed my dead name. (He did not.) "What was your name before all of this?"

It's hard to take the question seriously because I've always been Raine. I know what he is referring to, though. I'm transgender. He points to my beard and my chest, his eyes ablaze with a curiosity it isn't my job to sate. For my safety, I know I must answer with a modicum of severity.

"That doesn't matter," I respond, carrying the same energy I've always brought to those who questioned my name.

In this moment, even though I am staring down an aggressive, drunk man twice my size, I feel lucky because my long relationship with my name gives me a head start to combat transphobia. I know how to stand up for myself and my identity–a skill many of my trans peers had to learn on the fly for the first time while experiencing all the confusion, fear, and uncertainty that comes with transitioning. Facing down this man, however, is a jarring experience. But I am ready for this.

He continues to plague my spouse and me with invasive questions, always coming back around to asking about our genitals.

"So, do you have a penis or a 'hoo-ha'?"

My spouse gets increasingly uncomfortable. I steel myself. My demeanor changes. I channel my name; the same power and peace that helped me leave my abusive family, survive homelessness, and build my life from scratch. I become the storm.

"Look, dude, I'm happy to talk with you about many things, but the answer to that question doesn't matter, so you won't be getting one."

He continues. "I'm just asking because I want to learn. You know, I'm just an old fuddy-duddy. I want to better myself."

111

I know that isn't true. He is the same type of man as the high school bullies that used to make a game out of trying to guess my dead name. He is plagued by a curiosity, and he's used to the world answering his every question.

I will not. I am Raine. While there is peace in my name, there is also power; thunder, lightning, and destruction that can scar you. I am something that makes you run for cover.

Fed up, I finally cut him off.

"You know, my man, Google is a wonderful tool if you want to do some research about trans people."

He has no power in this situation.

No one can hold power over me. I know my name.

He realizes he will not win whatever game he thinks we are playing. He takes his beer and leaves. We both let out the breath we didn't know we were holding. Once again, I thank my name for powering me through another hardship.

The sound of the rain;
The power of a storm;
The childlike release of jumping in puddles;
The destruction of a lightning strike;
The roar of thunder;

It is all a part of me. I carry that. In this world, which has so many ways in which it can strike you down or make you feel less than, I am blessed to know the importance of a name. I hope, with the deepest sincerity, that this Raine can help wash away someone else's hesitancy to claim their name the same way I claimed mine.

***

Raine Grayson (he/him) is a multi-genre storyteller who specializes in social action theatre and autobiographical nonfiction focusing on the trans and queer experience. His work has been featured in over a dozen publications and festivals and he's had storytelling engagements with organizations like The Trevor Project. He currently works for non-profit theatre company TMI Project (tmiproject.org) running writing workshops, editing, and producing "true storytelling" performances that transform everyday people's stories into monologues.

18 | The Summer Nap by Sky Khan

We traveled tens of thousands of miles, following the tire treads that roamed before us. The city in our rearview mirror, we were Mother Nature seekers.

This summer, I wanted to master the road trip. Master my ego. Eradicate FOMO, and persistent restlessness. I wanted to be satisfied and maybe reassured. Would I be missed?

I gathered our four children. Five hours to escape the western half of Texas. From there we'd go North. An epic road trip. Maybe I'd finally write that book that kept slipping into "next year." Most of all, I wanted my health back.

We had spent the year inside. Stuck in cement buildings. Innate structures of various shapes and sizes that bore witness to our human efforts and the tragedy we faced that year. Our apartment walls encased a handful of awards and trophies, our decisions (both good and bad), echoes of past arguments, some heartbreak, and our hope.

During the year, I yearned for the outside world. But I was stuck. Hours spent in a chair, punctured by hypodermic needles, tethered to IV bags, soaked with poisonous drugs. To pass the time, I powered through podcast after podcast. *The Moth, Imagined Life, Oprah's Super Soul, Old Time Radio, Help! I Have a Teenager.* I bounced around, depending on my mood.

On January first, I was in the chair again, writing an anti-resolutions list. There were four bad habits that I would part with this year. If I could make it through the year.

A podcast played in one ear, but I had tuned out. A nurse flicked the IV tubing to drive bubbles back to the drip, and I took in a deep inhalation. Suddenly, I could hear. One sentence from the podcast stood out, louder than the words that came before.

"You will live for the moments that can't be put into words."

I exhaled. The sentence imprinted in my subconscious. A new awareness, a clue that there was something more that I needed to do.

I could put the hospital behind me. I wouldn't be defined by this. The hair would grow back. At this moment, a wave of clarity struck me. I knew what I had to do this summer. I would take my four kids and my drained and disfigured body, and we'd travel far away from cement. We would seek new experiences. The kinds that would leave us speechless. We wouldn't be able to describe what we'd seen to anyone who wasn't there.

Under swollen clouds in Big Sky country, drops of water slashing diagonally through the heat, flickering mirages rose from long straight stretches of road. My lungs took deeper, full breaths. The enormous weight lifting, I shed layers of skin.

It was finally June. Four kids and I piled into a rented sedan. Our teenager sat up front with me, our youngest was sandwiched in between the middles. We roamed. Crisscrossing forward and back on paths already explored by other seekers before us. Texas to North Dakota, Washington to Alaska, Oregon to Florida, The Carolinas to New England, our car became the consistent home base during the journey. I wanted to ace the road trip, to accomplish something noteworthy. I wanted to inspire. Or maybe be inspired. I wanted to recognize myself again on this odyssey.

The surgery left cavities and had disfigured my core. We strayed from the path and painted mud from a dried riverbed on our stomach and legs. We wore one shirt all week long. We ate meals completely out of cans. We didn't do dishes. We were wild people in the wild.

We tiptoed in forests. The numbing feeling of pins and needles in my feet cushioned every step I took, a side effect of the hospital treatment. If footsteps had ever pressed into these remote parts of our country, there was no longer any evidence.

We hugged trees and addressed a flat tire. Sat by campfires and took selfies with people who became our friends. We lost reception and lost our maps. We cried over the lack of privacy, argued about who's turn it was to make breakfast, we eventually found our way again.

I made the decision to stay unplugged. We sang, told scary stories, and beat on drums purchased at a roadside gift shop. We bonded over new soda flavors like grass and Bob Ross and meditated inside caves. We played endless games of twenty-one questions, and I kept notes of hilarious things that were said. There were a lot of revelations and a lot of musings about life. Kids really do say the funniest things.

"The teen years are like taking your first steps ... into the real world."

"Daddy is fifty? He is growing up too fast!"

"Am I worrying about something that is harmless?"

"Can you smell love?"

"We can't say y'all anymore, we're in New York."

I sent up prayers and prayed to the flame within. I plunged into cold water, and the chill shocked my numb core and eased the immobility on my left side. I felt more like myself. Maybe I would make it. We drove on.

The bar was set high, but I was determined to get a straight-A report card if someone ever evaluated our road trip. This would be the perfect road trip. We'd go to all the right places, skipping nothing, ignoring not a single roadside attraction, and collecting as many experiences as possible.

Stories, encounters, landmarks, all gathered at a frantic pace. The podcast that had inspired this journey had never mentioned how many amazing, indescribable moments one could have. We used sleds to descend mounds of desert at White Sands National Park, borrowed boots to ride ponies through Tombstone, Arizona, and scaled the red rock canyons of Moab, Utah. We ran through the spray of erupting geysers, tried delicious appetizers on Best of the

U.S. lists, and captured funny photos by World's Largest roadside attractions.

Unfortunately, there was always a looming deadline on this trip. The upcoming school year was weeks away. So, I increased the pace. I applied the busyness of our city life to the pace of our summer road trip. How much more could we fit in? Every day I took us as near to the edge of exhaustion as we could go before crashing at a highway exit motel or Airbnb.

Somewhere in Idaho, in a small one-room cabin barely large enough for the five of us, I landed in bed. Miles of endless, flat farmland surrounded us. Exotic chickens, peacocks, and curious goats roamed the property.

The kids played outside the cabin while I reached temps of 104. Consumed by intense visions, everything was suspended for one day. I slowed down to zero miles per hour. I shed more skin.

The aftermath of a virus that reprogrammed my entire body left me with questions. Why did I glorify busyness? Why was I teaching our young children to value noise? Distractions?

The next day, I stepped out of the cabin and squinted at the rising sun. I looked at our happy children playing in the dirt with sticks. What a remarkable experience to pause for one day. Nothing fell apart, even if I didn't rush to fix it or address it in some way. Instead, I rested.

I had been exhausted for years. It was at least a decade since I paused to honor my body. Our children only ever saw a frantic person on the go.

I thought about what I was willing to experience going forward. As I climbed back to health, I would place guidelines that defined what I was willing to experience. The loving expression of a nap would not be radical or profound. I could be a role model for our family.

Raw, vulnerable, shiny, and new. I was open hearted and ready to get back on the road.

117

Our pace was much slower on the way home. My youngest daughter passed her hand over my fuzzy head where new hair sprouted. This life is a progression, not an exercise in perfection. A rested body can better appreciate the moments that can't be put into words.

At a truck stop, I gathered my children in a tight group hug. Nap day would become a thing for us. Every summer, we declared that one full day in bed, in our pajamas, would make it on the schedule.

As I held my kids close, I realized I wouldn't be missed after all. I would be right here.

***

Sky Khan lives in Texas Hill Country with her best friend Ben, their two sons and two daughters. Learn more at skykhan.com.

19 | Rolling Stock by Nina Smith

I still remember it like it was yesterday: at the boardroom meeting with the Freddie Mac team, at the exact moment I realized I just couldn't do it anymore. After all the effort I had put into rising through the ranks of both school and industry, I practically had scars on my hands from all the glass ceilings I broke along the way. On that day, however, I had enough. After putting forward a revolutionary new proposal that would allow us to collect delinquent debt more efficiently by taking individual debtors to criminal court, all I got in response was crickets.

Bill coughed into his sleeve, "You, uh, you must really be gunning for that promotion, huh?"

I heard Chuck mutter under his breath, "She's gonna need it to pay for that divorce."

"Yeah, but the higher ups will never take her seriously unless she puts more skin in the game, if ya know what I mean," Dave chortled, gesturing slyly to the conservative cut of my blouse.

More silence.

I was crestfallen. I said nothing, just ran sobbing from the room. I'd been treated this way throughout my career, but I was spinning out. I didn't put all the effort into my doctorate at Yale, including nearly one hundred pages of writing for my thesis, to be belittled because I was a woman! I was more successful than most of the men in that boardroom, anyway. It was time to move beyond the world of high finance and discover another passion in a realm where I could truly be recognized.

I'd tried everything I could to be the best version of myself those past few months: I was eating healthily, roller skating to work instead of driving, even trying to meditate for at least a few minutes each night before bed. When I got home from work that horrid day,

I tossed my helmet, knee pads, elbow pads, and wrist guards on the floor as soon as I entered my condo and threw myself on the couch, sobbing endlessly. My loving chihuahua, Dale, curled up in the small of my back.

I started roller skating seriously in elementary school after my stepmom took my sister and me to see a touring run of Starlight Express at the Chicago Theatre in 1990. My sister didn't get it, but the spectacle enthralled me. On the walk home, I told my stepmom that was what I wanted to do with my life. I wanted to be a professional roller skater/singer/train engine.

She laughed and said, "Just wait until you're older. That stuff doesn't exist in the real world. For now, let's focus on taming that frizzy hair and straightening your front teeth. Otherwise, you'll never get a good man to marry you." She said things like this to me often, but I'd built up emotional knee pads to soften the blow.

Still, I had a few brushes with roller rink fame in my day. Once, I lied to my stepmom and told her I was going to sleep over at my friend Jennifer's house, but instead, Jen and I took the bus down to the South Side to see DJ Casper emcee at a run-down rink in Summit. He had a few catchy tracks, and I heard one he was workshopping a few years later on the radio: "The Cha Cha Slide."

I abandoned roller skating when I went to college. There would be no time for such frivolous activities if I were to succeed as a student at Yale University. Nevertheless, I held onto my beat-up Walkman over the years. After a tough test or a hard time at work dealing with misogynistic co-workers, my only solace was found in blasting Andrew Lloyd Webber showtunes from my roller skating days.

Dale snored softly next to me, but my head was spinning. All I could hear was the gruff voice of my coworker criticizing my outfit over and over as the dizzying scalar passages from "The Race is On," twisted back on themselves. I couldn't go back to the office the next day. I just couldn't.

***

Two weeks later, I was lacing up my skates at the Fleetwood Roller Rink, where I had just been hired as an instructor.

"Okay, class," I said to the gaggle of youths in front of me, who were busy chatting about the latest Pokemon cards and Eminem tunes.

"Class?" I tried again. "Class!?"

"SHUT UP!!!!"

That got their attention. "Thank you," I intoned. "Today we're going to be learning how to skate backwards."

Admittedly, it wasn't my dream job, but it paid the bills for me and Dale, and every night after my lessons, I could get out into the rink and show off my moves. I was a little "Rusty" with the Starlight Express routine I'd practiced in this very rink as a child, but the intricate choreography soon came back to me. Little did I know, I was in fact "train"-ing for what was going to be my big break.

A few months into the new job, I felt worn down. But my love for skating never fizzled out. However, the children kept getting on my nerves, and since I had perfected my moves, I had nothing to work on in the evenings. Rather than breaking another glass ceiling, I had plateaued. I thought returning to my old passion would put my troubles behind me, but maybe it was time to pump the brakes. I'd been running from my schizophrenia long enough. Skating was my medicine, but maybe the dose wasn't quite right.

But that night, in the locker room, everything changed when I saw a flyer on the wall: "Seeking Experienced Roller skaters for Touring Theatre Production."

It was Starlight Express!

Could it be …? How many roller skating musicals could there be? I tore down the entire flyer so nobody else got a chance to take the spot that I deserved so much.

121

No one at the audition would think twice about hiring me based on my skirt length–we all would wear leggings underneath them!

The auditions went smoothly. Starlight Express answered me with yes! I got the part. Thanks, in part, to my campaign of tearing down posters at rinks all across Chicagoland. The rehearsals started right away, and they were often grueling. After four weeks, it was finally opening night.

I peeked through the curtains a few minutes before the show was about to go on. I knew my old office sometimes bought tickets to the Nederlander Theatre for partners or visiting clients. I wondered if anybody was sitting in the usual block in the seventh row. Sure enough, there were a couple of my former coworkers sitting there. And not just any coworkers, but some of the sexist ones I'd battled with at my job. I was nervous about performing in front of them in pivotal scenes with Dinah, the dining car, and Buffy the Buffet Car. Would they recognize me?

Fortunately, once the house lights went down, and the skates went on, all the voices in my head stopped criticizing me and cheered me on. I settled perfectly into my part. I wasn't just acting as a train; I was a train, and I was ready to smash through the glass curtain and roll over anything in my path. I only fell over on stage once, which occurred because another dancer who played one of the Hip Hoppers knocked me off my balance. It was not intentional, but he tended to be one of those aggressive alpha male types in rehearsals. Overall, I felt it was quite the triumph! I was ecstatic. I felt as though I had finally reached the top of the emotional and career success pyramid, even though roller skating wasn't originally my intended path.

At the end of the show, the audience clapped so loudly it was deafening. My dance crew came out toward the end, and as I skated along the apron, I was careful to make eye contact with the creeps in the seventh row. I think they recognized me because their hoots and hollers instantly melted to embarrassment as I looked their way.

That's right, I thought, Starlight Express? Answer. Me. Yes. I'm living my dream right now. What have you done in the last two years? They didn't find me after the show. It didn't surprise me that they were intimidated to face me.

I've never quite been able to capture the rush I felt during that performance any time since. That experience was the culmination of everything I had been hoping for and working towards since I was a small child, dazzled by the theatrical display of singers on skates pretending to be trains. All I can dream of now is that one day the good old Express will make another stop in Chicago. And on a separate note, I'm eagerly awaiting the local musical production of Xanadu …

Moral of the story: Even in the dire face of sexism, a real woman can accomplish anything if she puts her mind to it.

***

Nina Smith, PhD, is a former credit analyst for Freddie Mac and a current consultant in the field of corporate ethics. She got her doctorate from Yale University in Women's, Gender, and Sexuality Studies, focusing on the representations of women in the theatre. For a brief period in her life, she also performed in several Broadway in Chicago productions. She currently resides in Chicago with several chihuahuas.

20 | Waking Up by Gavin Ross

It's been years, but there's a hallway I remember here, past that door and the one beyond it. The memory is like wood smoke or the odor of warm toast; just beyond being clearly seen or smelled, but dimly perceived and lingering still, as if it's something I've forgotten and now struggle to recall. Behind the doors is the ICU, the ten or so single rooms arranged around a central nursing station. Mine is the third one in, set in the corner on the left near the back. Its' window looks out onto the road and the cars and beyond that to the open fields of the park, green and inviting.

But the distance hurts my head, and the blinds have the taste of dust choking me down—between the light and the sky and the faded white slats it's all too much so I keep my eyes closed most of the time. There are too many things to see otherwise. Anything outside the hospital seems too far away, like a memory replayed in my mind so many times as I try to convince myself it's real and fail continuously.

There's people here, too—real, actual living people, but far more interesting are the dead people, the ghosts gliding by the other window, the inside window I'm not sure is there at all, their legs and feet motionless a good six inches off the floor. If only I could see their feet, which I cannot. But I know they're there, floating.

Of course, they aren't real ghosts. My brain tells me this and I repeat it to the real people I talk to, the doctors and the nurses. They must be actual people, I tell them, because I don't believe in ghosts; ghosts aren't real. But my eyes keep seeing these people who aren't real, with bodies too still for pedestrian motion, their faces blank, their lips unmoving, their cold dead eyes staring off into the distance or maybe into the past and then vanishing behind the wall or maybe through it as quickly as they appeared. A parade of them all damn day long, and when I tell the real people about it nobody tells me if they are actually there or not, so I never really know. They're so bothersome, coming and going with no regard for my tired eyes, my brain forced to accept their presence whether they are there or simply imagined. Even shutting my eyes doesn't stop them because when I open them again, there they are, stupidly existing, floating in and out, back and forth, endlessly.

Stupid too, are the questions I have to answer, over and over. A dozen doctors a day asking, "Where are you?" and "What hospital are you in?" and "What year is it?" And the dumbest of all, "Who's the President of the United States?"

Who cares, I think. They annoy me with all their questions.

When my wife comes in, she bites her lip, holds my hand and asks, "Do you know who I am?"

"Of course, I know," I respond irritably, "Why do you keep asking?"

But a few minutes ago, I didn't, and in a few minutes more maybe I won't.

I see many things here, like the walls dripping with green glitter—was that this time? No, that was another time, in a different hospital room. It was the drugs that caused that particular hallucination. Now it's just me, my brain swollen from bacterial meningitis, struggling to figure everything out. Posters and signs that make no sense because every time I blink, the letters rearrange themselves, making reading impossible. At first, this is amusing and sort of fascinating. But soon it begins to hurt and is distracting, so I cannot look at them, teasing, vexing me with their boggled nonsense and words I can't decipher.

How is it that I find myself back in this place for the third time in a year at only age thirty-eight? Most of my teen years were spent in places like this, in cancer wards and radiation suites, in waiting rooms full of sad eyed people, their faces masking pain and fear. My chest and abdomen are still crisscrossed with the scars that mark the

125

price of survivorship; medicine bottles still rattle in my pants pockets. I was dying and then somehow, I stopped. Through the grace of medical science and sheer stubbornness, I refused to die and got on with living again, for many years.

Then the dying started anew, when my newly discovered genetics caught up with me and a tumor formed in my spine, thanks to a random gene called SDHB that I inherited from my mother. Hell of a family legacy, that gene. I talked with my surgeon on the eve of the operation, on my thirty-eighth birthday, with my infant daughter in my lap.

"What if we leave it there in my spinal column, at the second and third cervical vertebrae in my neck? What will happen then?"

"You'll stop breathing and die," he replied with his profession's characteristic brusqueness.

So out it came, and my left side has never felt the same since. It tingles always, cheek to arm to leg and down to my smallest toes, sometimes a tickle, sometimes like needles. The meds help, but I get weak and often drop things. And if I get too tired, my left hand doesn't work right, and I can't rely on it to listen to my brain.

But six months later, six months of pain and green glittering walls and trying to prove to the world and mostly to myself that I could still do my job and still be a father, still do it all somehow, I woke up back in the hospital. I found myself there after an excruciating week of headaches blinding me, ice picking my temples. There's no reason the meningitis infection happened, just bad luck, they tell me. I was driving seven hours earlier, no problem except for a headache. But then I was raving, frightening my wife and children. My dad drove me to the hospital as I rapidly forgot who I was. Once I got there, it got worse; I was clumsily attacking the staff, put in five-point restraints, tied to the bed. I remember trying to head butt a nurse, several inches shorter than me, but I was so uncoordinated I could hardly stand. But that is all.

126

That was the first time. Six months after that, my wife brought me back again. I don't remember anything of this one, but apparently she had to sit on my chest while I was on the stretcher in the emergency room to stop me from pulling out my IV lines and the catheter in my penis. I woke up after spending three days in a coma and asked my wife repeatedly, "Was it meningitis again?"

Every time she said, "Yes, it was."

I always had the same response, "Damn, I fucking hate meningitis."

Days later when I was out of bed and walking, when the ghosts had gone away and I could read again, my brain not so infected, I'd walk through the wards and into the unsteady elevator, down to the first floor and into the hallway. I'd walk past the doors in front of the corridor of my ICU, beyond the gift shop, to reach the Tim Hortons. It was the good Tim Hortons, the one where I could get the best coconut donuts, the white ones, not the brown. I'd eat two a day, and a small hot chocolate, shuffling along with ghosts real and imagined, those remembered from my fevered mind a few days earlier and those that have died here maybe and left behind an echo of their souls, memories sliding together piece by piece like a jigsaw puzzle.

My daughters couldn't see me at first; that was not allowed. Apparently, I'd forgotten I even had daughters, although I don't remember this. When I do remember, remember that I have two, the fear of what could have been lost nearly drowns me. For them I would do anything, but if I had died, what would they have lost, living a life with a wound that never heals? I've nothing to lose if I'm dead, but those left behind, they're the ones who have the most to lose, remembering what is missing every day. My kids and my wife with her stupid questions, "Who am I?" she asks. Just because I forgot her once, and then again, a second time six months later, doesn't she know who she is, to remind herself? What would her life have been like?

Now years have passed and I'm back for an outpatient appointment and I walk these same warm fuzzy halls, the memories projected on my mind like an old sheet pinned to the wall in flickering eight-millimeter film, cloudy and grainy, speckled with spots and with age. Strangely, no fear walks with me here, in this place I have known. I smile and want only to linger, to recall everything I had forgotten and remembered and then forgotten again. The ghosts and the words and the random lady in a bee costume who was never really there at all, except in my eyes watching her dancing, dancing for hours, real as my wife, more real than my children—I could never hear her music. What should be believed? The things we see or the things we know to be true?

It's history now, a jumble of images and experiences I couldn't control, or even make sense of. But what toll has it taken on me? Trying to describe a brain injury, let alone two brain injuries, is difficult. Trying to describe the mushiness of thinking, the conscious effort of making thoughts flow coherently, and of failing, again and again, and how when I get worn out things shut down, physically, cognitively, emotionally. Stuff gets dropped and lost, the tingles become jabs, the left side of my body seems detached and feels wrong, like it's not really mine but grafted on somehow, quite poorly. I have to massage and beat that side with my fist, just to make it feel right, but it never does. The hearing loss from the brain injuries is the easiest thing to explain and to fix—hearing loss runs in my family anyway. Mine came on faster, but once my aids are in, the forgotten bird sounds and background soundtrack to life is beautiful. The other things—the forgetfulness, the blank memory spots, the emotional volatility I struggle to keep in check, things I don't even notice but my wife does. These are difficult things—hard to define and even harder to live with.

It's been a remarkable recovery though—I never had to relearn to walk, or to speak. I'm incredibly lucky to survive both meningitis one and two and still have a wonderful life, complete with a third daughter, all blond curls and boundless energy, the chance to see the sunshine and feel the rain and watch the three of them dance, learn, live, grow. I can walk, talk, drive a car. Looking at me, you'd never know what I've lost; never know how close I'd come to losing my family and myself.

But I know, every single day, I know. I don't think the same; the way thoughts are processed and information gets pushed from one neuron to the next is a physical effort, to have things line up like they should. The strain and fatigue make it too difficult to do the job I loved, working with children in hospitals, many of them with brain injuries, tumors, even meningitis sometimes. Life is funny that way.

All these things, all that's happened, I experience once again as I walk this hospital hallway, past the door and the one beyond that. There, the Tim Hortons is still there, but they don't have the good donuts today—there's a pandemic on, and pandemics are not a good time for donuts, among other things. Years have gone by, but everything's the same here in this hidden pocket of resistance against the ever-impending specter of death. The patients still hobble along, their IV poles softly rumbling, wheels softly squeaking, the dust in the carpets and the shining floors and the bathrooms that get cleaned twice daily. People live and die here, while outside this building, I've watched my three girls grow up. I've combed their unruly hair into messy ponytails, taught them how to ride bicycles and play hockey and light campfires.

Visiting this place again brings back so much that still doesn't fit into the boxes of my mind, square pegs in round holes, nothing filed away neatly. After all these years, and after fighting so much, I realize what was lost and what was gained here. In the end, I survived. I was changed irrevocably, but I survived and walked out the front doors and into my daughters' arms. These hospital walls should be a place of terror but there's a soft comfort here, where everything is still the same, the halls and doors and the room with the ghosts and the memories of the window and the straps around

129

my wrists tying me down to keep me from hurting myself or somebody else. All is here, right where I left it.

***

Gavin Ross has lived an interesting life as a writer, health care professional, and father of three from Toronto, Ontario. He is also a childhood cancer survivor, a brain injury survivor, and the parent of children with disabilities. After stops in Calgary, Vancouver, Philadelphia, and Adelaide, Australia, he now lives eighty-six kilometers (fifty-three miles) from where he was born. Life is funny that way. Previous publishing credits include *Freefall* and *Fertile Ground.*

21 | Morgan by Lee Roscoe

Eighteen months ago, I said goodbye to Morgan, my closest comrade. Morgan had been in my life for decades. He was there for me in good times, bad times, births, deaths, celebrations, funerals, weddings, and always, always there in my loneliest moments. No questions asked.

Morgan didn't die. I cut Morgan out of my life. I know he's still out there and would return to me in a moment's notice. And even though I made the right decision, making the loss stick will take a lifetime of reckoning.

I think most people know Morgan, or at least they have heard of him. But most people wouldn't recognize him unless I include his title. It's Captain. Captain Morgan. A prominent member of the rum family. Eighteen months ago, I cut Captain Morgan out of my life. I had to. Morgan had taken over and was controlling me.

But it didn't use to be that way.

My relationship with Morgan started innocently enough. When I was twelve, my sister and her husband took me to Jamaica with them. During the day, they would instruct me to say I was eleven, so that I could get on excursions for free. At night, my sister put makeup on me so I could get into the bars with them.

One night, my brother-in-law offered me a sip of his drink. It was Captain Morgan mixed with coke. It was sweet, spicy, and delicious. I fell in love. But I knew a relationship with Morgan would be wrong and impossible at that age. But I always recalled him fondly and vowed to find him when I was a bit older.

I briefly forgot about him when I was in high school. As a teenager, I drank what was around. My parent's liquor cabinet provided me with Tom Collins and Galliano turned a screwdriver into a delicious Harvey Wallbanger. When I made new friends after a school transfer, those girls liked wine, so I drank that most often. However, none of us seemed to understand anything about the proper amount one should drink, and that lack of education left me praying to the porcelain Gods most nights. And each headachy morning arrived with a vow to never drink again. But by the time the next party started, those meaningless promises were long forgotten.

Having outgrown fruity drinks in my twenties, Vodka took over in a massive way. I drank Russian vodka straight up, but also vodka martinis and the occasional gimlet. I was married in those days and whenever we went out on a Saturday night, I usually ended up sleeping on the bathroom floor because I would be sick all night. My husband would say, "I don't know why you can't stop at two."

I always marveled at that comment and wondered, who stops at two? It was a foreign concept to me. Those next days, it was always late in the afternoon, after abdicating my motherly responsibilities, that I could formulate words, always the same ones, "What did we do last night?" I couldn't remember because of the blackouts.

Vodka and I had a major falling out when I found myself in the dog run smoking a cigarette, trying to hide it from my family. When I awoke the next morning and realized that I spent the night smoking in shit, I left Vodka for good. I also gave up all alcohol for three-and one-half years.

But then Morgan came back into my life. Captain and coke. Sweet, spicy, delicious and with less alcohol by volume, Morgan never, never made me sick. Morgan was the answer.

I took Morgan everywhere because he was always welcome at parties, that fun little friend most people forgot about and were happy to see again. He always fit in. The life of the party. But mostly, he made me feel good about myself. Morgan gave me confidence; he made me brave and likeable and talkative in social situations.

During Covid, Morgan was there for me during Zoom drinks with my friend Debbie. We would have a zoom call several times a week around 5 p.m. in the evening. Morgan was my only companion during lockdown. Morgan made me happy and less lonely. I loved to pour Morgan into a vintage cocktail glass with lots of ice and clink the cubes. Morgan was happiness.

But then he started making demands. Morgan insisted on coming out daily, whether zooming or not. At first, I was alright with that because he made me happy every day. But it wasn't long before 5 p.m. turned into 3 p.m. I figured it was okay, because working from home, no one knew, and I wasn't that busy. Morgan and I were in a serious relationship. We were happy in our little bubble.

When the vaccinations made getting together possible, I went to see my son in Vegas. I stayed at a hotel and would have several Captain and Cokes before he picked me up for dinner. Morgan felt it best that my children not know how heavily involved we were. From there, I went on a vacation with Debbie, and she complained Morgan interfered with our evenings.

Morgan insisted we hide our relationship. When I met friends for dinner, I always got there early to meet Morgan at the bar.

Soon, I started waking up with headaches. I vowed I wouldn't see Morgan that night, but come evening, Morgan was clinking in my glass. Morgan took control, telling me when and where we would meet. He became insistent in a way that frightened me. When I tried to bargain, he would not take no for an answer.

Every night was the same: Drink. Every morning was the same: Headaches and spilling the remainder of last night's bottle down the drain.

When I tried to cut Morgan out of my life, he showed up everywhere: grocery stores, Target, convenience stores, gas stations. Always out there, always nearby, stalking me.

I went to a party and Morgan was there looking at me, beckoning in his sly way. He was next to the non-alcoholic punch, mocking me. I went into the other room, but I felt his strong pull.

On Mother's Day 2022, I had champagne with my daughter at brunch, but alone in my apartment at 5 p.m., Morgan insisted on making an appearance. The next morning, I admitted I was powerless over him. And if I wanted to take my power back and have some control over that life, there was only one way to get it.

That day, I found an Alcoholics Anonymous meeting in my neighborhood. And the people in that meeting helped me realize Morgan was not the problem. The problem was me. That day, as if by magic, Morgan was instantly banished in a way that I could never have accomplished on my own.

Today, after eighteen months of sobriety, I feel healthier, both physically and mentally, and I am completely honest. When a doctor asks me how much alcohol I consume, I no longer lie. My relationships are better because I am listening more, talking less, and not judging others. And I'm not focused on finding, concealing, or battling Morgan.

Sure, Morgan made me happy, but that happiness was fleeting, and came at a price. It cost me money, illness, solitude, and my self-esteem. My happiness now is consistent, real, and sincere.

I made the right decision to cut Morgan out of my life, but making the loss stick will take a lifetime of reckoning. One day at a time.

***

Lee Roscoe wishes to remain anonymous.

22 | Crossroads and Crescendos by Anne E. Beall

I loathed my job. It was as if everyone at the company had taken the same hallucinogenic drug, while I was the lone individual popping an aspirin. Each day felt like a descent into the twilight zone, where everyone but me shared the same reality.

The company was a traditional market-research firm. The owners found my background in cutting-edge research appealing. They dangled the lure of an equity-track position where I could be a part owner someday. It seemed like an amazing opportunity.

But have you ever been seized by that nagging sensation that something isn't right? That feeling plagued me during the interview and every working day after. The firm felt stuck in the 1970s, just like the office décor. My desk, a massive chunk of metal and faux wood, bore the marks of years of abuse. The walls bore scars from cleaning carts repeatedly scuffing against them, and the faded carpet was marred by one too many coffee spills.

One Monday morning after working there for a year, I trudged into the office feeling an unsettling, nauseous feeling. I often felt that way on Mondays, secretly wanting to be sick to escape the day. A colleague walked by, giving me a fleeting look of pity, which I found puzzling. Then the two owners told me to come to their office.

"We've decided to terminate your position," they declared when I sat down.

"Why?" I asked.

"Well, the firm isn't doing as well as it did last year. And frankly, we've not been happy with your performance."

"Really? I've brought in new business and more than covered my salary. We've had clients sending you letters about how happy they are …"

"Well, you need to leave. You have thirty minutes to get your stuff and leave. Anyway, I'm sure you understand."

"Actually, I don't. And if you're looking for me to make you feel better about your decision, I'm afraid I can't help you there."

With twenty-six minutes left on the clock, I hastily packed a few things and stepped out of that oppressive environment for the last time. Riding the city bus, dressed in my work clothes with a box cradled in my lap and a briefcase beside me, I felt as if the world knew I'd just lost my job. It seemed as if the word "loser" was plastered across my forehead. As I gazed out through the bus's smudged window, watching Michigan Avenue drift by, everything felt bleak.

When I arrived home, my husband looked surprised and asked what happened.

"I'm not sure. All I know is they hired me so they could do innovative things, but every time I suggested conducting a study online or building their website, they balked. It was so frustrating. Every single day."

"Maybe you could get your job back at BCG?" He suggested.

"I tried a while ago," I said and then looked down. I hadn't told him that my former boss acted as if she didn't know me when I emailed. Her rebuff was too embarrassing.

I'd left a respected role at the Boston Consulting Group, where I genuinely enjoyed working with sharp, driven colleagues. The office was decked out in light wood furniture, and everything was in pristine condition. Even the restrooms exuded elegance with their marble finishes.

I looked at my husband. "I'm kind of relieved I never have to go back there."

In the subsequent weeks, I relentlessly hunted for a job. Engaging with recruiters, scouring job postings, and networking became my full-time endeavor. There were few positions, and I was over or under-qualified for them. I sunk into a brief depression.

I needed to reinvent myself. During those couple of months without a job, I reflected on how a body-language seminar I'd created at BCG had been very popular. I told my husband I wanted to start a training company that helped people read nonverbal communication.

"I don't think there's any money in that," he responded.

I would not be dissuaded and launched my business. My "office" was an old, rust-colored armoire that transformed into a makeshift desk in my bedroom. Although the phone buzzed unless positioned just right, it hardly bothered me. After all, I was now my own boss!

My days morphed into marathon sessions as I poured heart and soul into my enterprise: reaching out to contacts, sending countless cards and emails, crafting my website, and attending networking events. Finally, I landed my first training session at a major bank.

At the end of the training session, the Vice President who hired me said, "I'm not sure that I learned anything new. How is this body-language training?"

My explanations were met with silence.

But I continued. I relentlessly pursued potential clients, making cold calls to complete strangers. Offering private in-office training sessions, I hoped to pitch my services. After many meetings, I conducted several training courses for Northwestern Mutual Financial Network. But I made very little money. Sleep eluded me, and I'd often wake in the night, pondering how to make my business sustainable. And a significant realization dawned on me: I did not enjoy teaching body language.

Around this time, a colleague from BCG asked if I would be interested in doing a market-research study for the private-equity firm where he worked. They wanted to use market research to determine if they should invest in a company. I gladly agreed and our study showed that an investment in this business would have been a mistake. That company was Blockbuster. My business took off. Project after project started to come in. I went from being in the red to the black. I realized I loved doing market research for myself. And I really loved working with my clients who appreciated my innovative approaches to their business problems. My business had been reinvented from a body language company to a market-research firm.

After six months, I had enough money to pay rent on a tiny office downtown. Occupying a quaint space on the thirteenth floor, I often felt lonely, but I kept at it. I wanted so badly to succeed.

The 2008 recession hit hard. Phone calls and emails went unanswered, and a cloud of anxiety loomed over me. Having committed to a two-year lease with no incoming projects, sleep became difficult again. The shame of failing after telling everyone that I "owned my own business" weighed heavily on my mind.

During this period, I won a modest project with a bank that would keep the business going for a few months. They wanted to understand why customers were over drafting their checking accounts. My work comprised individual interviews with chronic over drafters in various cities across the U.S. In one instance, a female client took offense when I didn't respond to her query as quickly as she wanted. She tried to have me removed from the project. But the main male client defended me. His support was initially reassuring, but that sentiment quickly shifted when he pressured me to join him at the hotel bar. There, he insisted I consume a few shots. After excusing myself to use the restroom, I was taken aback when he suddenly tried to kiss me as I stepped into a deserted hotel hallway outside the women's room.

"No, no. I'm married," I said.

"And so am I," he replied with a chuckle.

I exerted every ounce of effort to distance myself from him, even feigning illness to retreat to my hotel room. However, throughout the rest of the project, he seemed to be ever-present, especially when I was alone. On the last day, he unexpectedly arrived at my hotel room, citing a wish to use the hotel gym and then to shower in my suite. He tried to kiss me again, and he hinted I owed him. I told him I just couldn't do this, and he left annoyed. Following that assignment, I never received another project from that bank, and I couldn't help but feel his influence played a part. Had I been more accommodating, perhaps my journey through the recession might have been smoother.

Sexism has undeniably colored my experience in this industry. More often than not, I was the lone woman in a room filled with male senior executives. Many times, I faced patronizing men who ignored my research, gave unwanted advice on my business, or asked for discounts because we were a small, woman-owned company. Despite these challenges, I consistently held my ground, always trusting in my capabilities, my firm, and the superior quality of our work.

During the recession, I wrote the book, *Strategic Market Research: A Guide to Conducting Research that Drives Businesses.* The book brought in new clients. Soon, my workload burgeoned, requiring me to hire employees. The team expanded gradually, and we moved to a plush ten-room suite, adorned with furnishings reminiscent of those at BCG: personal offices, a conference space, and a welcoming reception. We had gone from a single employee working out of a bedroom to a five-million-dollar business with sixteen employees.

Through my business, I connected with clients who taught me as much as I instructed them. My work took me all over the world: in India, I explored how local businesses adapted to digital platforms; in Japan, I assessed market reactions to new mattress innovations; and in Europe, I delved into the evolving landscape of cancer treatments. These business trips are some of the most cherished memories of my life.

When Covid struck in 2020, it required a recalibration. Some of our projects vanished, leading us to shift our focus and reduce our staff. Now, we function with a streamlined team, doing only projects that align with our core strengths. We take pride in the long-standing relationships we've built with clients, some of whom have been with us for nearly two decades.

I have also become affiliated with Women in Research, an organization dedicated to supporting women in my field. Over the past few years, I've mentored many women, aiming to shield them from the profound loneliness I frequently felt, the relentless sexism I faced, and the challenges that come with being a female entrepreneur. It's the most gratifying role I can envision at this juncture in my career.

When I think about my business, the overwhelming surge of pride I feel is almost palpable. As we mark twenty years of a prospering business and an exceptional team, my heart swells with immense gratitude and satisfaction.

A while ago, I crossed paths with one of the owners who had dismissed me at my prior job. I greeted him warmly, remembering our shared history. While he walked past without acknowledgment, I realized I bore no ill-will. In fact, had he stopped, I would have thanked him. Embarking on the entrepreneurial path transformed me. I am deeply appreciative and grateful for every twist and turn in my journey.

***

Anne E. Beall is an award-winning author whose books have been featured in *People Magazine, Chicago Tribune, Toronto Sun, Hers Magazine, Ms. Career Girl,* and she's been interviewed by NBC, NPR, and WGN. She has also published in numerous many literary journals. Beall received her PhD in social psychology from Yale University and is the founder of the strategic market-research firm, Beall Research.

23 | Caught Between Two Worlds by Jeannine Kacmar

I didn't pay attention to the phone ringing. In our household of fourteen, there was always lots of noise and someone else to answer the phone. Mom and dad had left for their Friday date night. They were both in playful moods. Mom had even curled her hair and put on lipstick. My older sisters were getting ready to go out on their own dates and my younger sisters and brother and I had just settled down with a big bowl of popcorn to watch my favorite Christmas special, *Rudolph the Red-Nosed Reindeer*. This show was only broadcast once a year, and even though I felt I was a little too old at fifteen to be so excited for it, I didn't want to miss getting a jumpstart on the holiday.

Suddenly my older sister yelled at us to shut off the TV. "Something's wrong with mom!" she said as she hung up the phone. "Get dressed! We're going to the hospital!"

When we got to the ICU, a doctor stopped us by the door regarding the pack of us in our mismatched clothes and wide-eyed confusion. He said, "Your mother is very sick. We give her a one-percent chance to make it through the night. I suggest you each go in and say your farewells."

His words were a gut punch, and I blinked back tears of dread as I lined up in the hall outside her room with my eleven siblings. As I waited my turn to go inside, I heard my older sisters whisper the words "CPR" and "resuscitate." A knot in my gut grew tentacles wrapping themselves around my chest and throat, making it difficult to breathe. Mom was a nurse and sometimes brought me to the hospital to help with the patients on Bingo Night. I had seen what an illness could do to a person's body and mind, and I didn't want to see mom crumpled in a wheelchair, unable to think or speak. So, I

141

prayed over and over to myself, "Don't let her die, don't let her become a vegetable, please!"

My older sister turned to us as we waited our turn in line, and hissed out instructions, jabbing her finger at us for emphasis. "I don't want to see any of you crying. Go in, say bye to mom, and leave!"

I shuffled along in line, moving forward against my will. The door to the ICU opened, one of my sisters would be ushered in by hands from the other side of the door. The sounds from inside the room, urgent whispers, and beeping machines, silenced as soon as the door shut.

I felt like I was sitting in a roller coaster cart with that sense of impending doom as I clicked clacked up the track higher and higher, waiting for the drop. I knew the fall was coming, but all I could do was hold on tight and close my eyes.

The ICU door opened, and I was pulled inside for my turn. I noticed an accordion-like machine connected to the body in the bed, and for a split second, I was relieved to see that there must have been some mistake. Somehow, I got in the wrong line because I didn't recognize the body. The size and shape of it looked inflated, like a Macy's Thanksgiving Day Parade balloon. The swollen face was covered with a large breathing mask taped across the nose and mouth. The eyes were closed.

I was about to rejoice at this apparent mistake until I saw the mole on the face that belonged to the body strapped to the bed. On the only spot not covered by white tape was the mole on the chin that marked my mom, unmistakable, undeniable. I felt the roller coaster cart go over the edge of the track and begin to plummet, leaving me weightless for a split second. I could feel the scream coming, but remembered I was ordered not to cry. I needed to speak to mom to say goodbye, but could only watch the bloated body move in rhythm with the billows of that accordion machine.

I squeaked out, "Mom?"

Then, urgent hands pushed me out the door for the next person in line. "I love you!" was all I could shout out before I was back in the hallway as the door closed.

Mom lay in a coma, and I had to go home and resume my life, go to school, doctors' orders. I walked numbly through my days, desperately hanging onto the "one-percent chance" and feverishly prayed for her to live.

On the third day of her coma, mom woke up. At the hospital, dad sat next to mom's bed, perched on a stool too small for his large frame. When I entered the room, I noticed his strained smile and his eyebrows raised too high, like he was trying to pretend everything was normal. He spoke to mom in a voice a little too loud, as if she had a hearing problem, "This is one of your daughters, Ronnie, one of the twins!"

It took a few seconds before mom turned her head to look at me, and I wondered if her hearing really was damaged. When her eyes met mine, it was as if I was meeting a stranger. They saw me but didn't know me.

I knew why dad looked desperate because I felt that same look growing on my face.

Mom looked as if she either didn't hear a word dad said or didn't understand him. She didn't react to our forced smiles or greeting. She just lay there blinking her eyes like someone caught between two worlds, and she hadn't decided which one she wanted to be in.

I felt like I just arrived in a new land where the once familiar was outlandishly bizarre, a land where my mom was now the child. She had forgotten how to speak, how to feed herself, how to walk, and she didn't recognize her family. It was a place where medical words like "cerebral aneurysm" and "aphasia" explained the foreign topography and dictated the new look of my life.

I visited mom every day after school. Because mom's hands didn't work right, I showed her how to fit the spoon in her hand and how to lift it to her mouth to feed herself. Because she had forgotten

143

the alphabet and how to write letters and numbers, I wrote them out on lined paper for her to trace and I guided her hand over the familiar shapes.

Mom sweated with the effort of lifting her spoon or holding a pencil and I cheered when she succeeded. Yet, these simple movements exhausted her. She would sometimes become frustrated and angry or completely withdrawn when her mind and body didn't respond to her commands. The nurses told me depression was a common side effect of patients with brain damage. Yet, this side of mom was so different from the mom before the aneurysm, the mom who would light up a room with the smile in her eyes, whose first instinct upon greeting someone was a hug and a kiss, who could be heard singing about the house as she worked. This new sadness settled on her shoulders, making them slump and pulled her gaze to the floor. It kept her from looking up when people called her name. It arrived into our lives without invitation, and I dreaded the thought of having to get used to this unwelcome guest.

When working with mom, I was instructed by the nurses to wait patiently when she tried to speak. When she said, "close the door," but pointed to her coffee cup, I had to keep from jumping in with my guesses.

"Close the door? Are you cold, Mom? You want more coffee? You need a blanket? You thirsty?"

I thought with a futility I didn't yet know, that if I could take care of her every need, I could make everything better and life would get back to normal.

Despite all her challenges, mom continued to make progress and came home from the hospital on Christmas Eve. We traditionally celebrated Christmas Eve with a big holiday dinner prepared by mom, who had cooked all our meals while also teaching her daughters how to cook. Instead, we gathered around the table set with a meal prepared not by mom but for her. We crowded into the dining room, talking across the table, forks clinking on plates, carrying on as if life was normal again. But I saw mom from across the table staring down at her plate as if she couldn't hear any of us and was alarmed to see the unwelcome guest had followed her home.

All the kids continued to help mom with her recovery, working to refine the coordination she needed to walk.

We watched TV exercise guru Jack LaLane, and I'd join mom in toe touches and arm circles. Over time, she could keep up with him until he came to jumping jacks. A movement that seemed so simple to me would cause mom to be stuck with her arms up and legs out looking like a letter X, so I would pull down her arms one at a time and she would bring her feet back together, completing a jumping jack in piecemeal. It wasn't like Jack LaLane's, but we counted it a victory.

I walked alongside to steady her on the stairs as she practiced lifting her feet one step at a time. She eventually figured out how to climb a whole flight but only one stair at a time, like a child. We claimed it as a victory, too.

Her movements became more fluent in the kitchen when holding utensils, stirring pots, and cutting vegetables, but the frustration and anger continued to flare up unpredictably. One day, I was working in the kitchen with mom, who was standing at the cutting board when she picked up the brown-handled knife and screamed, "I should just kill myself with this knife!"

All I could do was stare back at her, blinking in shock and choking back tears. I had prayed and prayed for her to live, and now she wanted to die. I hated the dreaded depression and its cape of gloom that cast itself over us all, like it was greedier for more lives than mom's. Its darkness threatened to extinguish what light was left, and I was afraid for her and myself if we couldn't see a better tomorrow.

We carried on with her recovery and a little over a year after mom got sick, she was able to return to work as a nurse. We were

145

able to continue moving forward through the dark times, which gave me hope for the future. As a grown woman, looking back at this time in my life, I know those were some of my darkest days. As a fifteen-year-old in the thick of emotional trauma, I didn't know how those days would impact the rest of my life, but the lessons revealed themselves over time.

I saw that pain and suffering could happen when least expected, and I learned that having faith could help me endure. Years later, when my dad underwent a heart transplant, I once again faced the dark clouds of worry and doubt about his extensive recovery. But I remembered to focus beyond my fears to continue moving forward with him to regain his health.

I also learned that nothing in life is guaranteed, especially in the time I have with my family. When I became a mother with my own daughters, hellos and goodbyes held a significant weight. We became a family of hugs and kisses focusing on the simple acts of saying, "I love you." I want my girls to remember the good and preciousness of each day, no matter what comes along in life.

***

Jeannine Kacmar is a published writer who likes to bike ride with her husband, bake with her daughters, and gather with her eleven brothers and sisters and their families and share stories about growing up.

24 | Snow Day by Kellie D. Brown

My father drives me to school in his pickup truck and deposits me near the front door later than normal. Last night's televised news indicated that my county school system would operate on Snow Schedule today. Despite the superintendent's habit of changing his mind in the early morning hours as road conditions hadn't miraculously improved, no one at my house bothered to recheck the schedule. Unlike my mother, who would wait until I was inside, my father says goodbye and drives away. He doesn't notice that the parking lot is unusually sparse. No other cars parked there. No other children.

I make my way to the double doors and tug on the right one's handle. I try again with more force. It's locked. I look around just as a construction worker wearing work boots and overalls with a canvas jacket appears on an outdoor staircase that leads to an upper floor classroom. He notices me even though I'm small and hidden under my winter coat.

"What's going on?" he shouts down at me.

"The door is locked. I can't get in."

"Well, come in this way," he counters.

So, I do.

The warm building is a welcome relief from the frigid temperature. Only then, once I'm inside, do I experience a hint of wariness. My stomach knots, and my eyes dart around. I'm conscious of being in an enclosed space with a male stranger who is considerably bigger than he seemed before I mounted the stairs. I consider stepping back outside. But then the construction worker returns to his task, leaving me to find my second-grade classroom. However, when I cross the threshold of the classroom, instead of my cheerful teacher bustling around and other students preparing for the day, I encounter a vacant room, with the chairs still turned upside down on the tops of the desks as we had placed them the day before it snowed.

Even though the space is obviously empty, I call out in a frightened voice, "Mrs. Rutherford?"

All I hear is silence.

I spend a few minutes roaming around the classroom before exiting into the hallway. Fear renders my legs as shaky as a newborn fawn's, so I sit down on the bottom step of the closest stairwell. Bracing my elbows on my knees, I gaze down the long, empty corridor. I'm at school alone.

My fear quickly morphs into resolve, and it only takes a couple of minutes to devise a plan. I envision my grandparents' house, located in a subdivision behind the school. I can travel through the playground, around the Little League ball field, and emerge in their backyard. I push through the doors that hadn't allowed me entry. As soon as the cold air hits my face, I run.

The same construction worker who let me into the building calls, "Where are you going, little girl?"

I point behind the school, never breaking stride, and yell, "I'm going to my grandma's."

I make it through the large playground, with its obstacle course of equipment, and come to the wide ditch that runs alongside the Little League ball field. The ground is snow-covered, frozen solid beneath my little feet as I try to run in that ditch. My warm coat provides some protection, but the cold air stings my face, and tears gather in the corners of my eyes. I'm not wearing mittens. My arms hold my beloved Trapper Keeper notebook that I clasp tightly to my chest. It is my companion at home and at school with its brightly colored folders that I love to sort my papers into after making that satisfying sound as I rip open the Velcro cover flap. I know where I'm going. I can see it in the distance, but the house seems to grow no closer despite my pounding feet and heart.

The snow under my feet was loose and manageable at first, but now it's packed and slippery. One minute I'm upright making progress, and then I've fallen down. The Trapper Keeper pressed protectively to my chest takes the brunt of the forward plant. When I regain my footing in the icy ditch, I'm horrified to discover the notebook's shiny back cover is split. Then I'm running again. Through stinging tears, I see the open carport of my grandparents' home, and with relief, I dart in there and reach my finger toward the doorbell.

I jam my finger into the doorbell's lighted button several times in rapid succession, even though I know I'm breaking an important rule. We all know this one rule. Never ring the doorbell during the daytime. My grandmother has posted a sign above it for those who don't know.

DAYSLEEPER. DO NOT RING THE DOORBELL.

My grandfather works the graveyard shift as a foreperson at a textile mill. He is not always an ill-tempered man, especially when singing or playing the fiddle, but he is easily dissatisfied and has little tolerance for inconvenience. Nothing riles him more than being awakened. So, during the day, my grandmother tiptoes around the house and positions herself as a human shield against noise.

When the door opens and I glimpse her loving face, I cry and blurt out the whole story.

"Dad took me to school, but nobody was there. I didn't know what to do but come here. I ran all the way. I'm cold, and I fell down."

Mamaw responds, "Oh, sweetheart, come in and get warm."

She pulls me into her arms and then reaches for the phone to call her daughter, my mother. But there is no answer.

Within a few minutes, my hysterical mother bursts through the door. Having realized their mistake, my parents rushed to the school and that same construction worker recounted the story of a little girl running toward her grandmother's house. This situation would have

149

shaken most mothers, but my mother, with her chronic inability to cope with life, will not be able to deal with this in a way that puts my welfare front and center. With her arrival, I pivot from being upset about my ordeal to being distraught that I have upset her. At age eight, I am already well-practiced at executing this shift.

My mother's crying, screaming, and grabbing at me coalesces into a disordered blur. I feel my muscles and stomach clench as I try to figure out how to calm her quickly, how to convince her that everything is okay, so her latest "scene" can pass. As usual, my father stands removed and ineffectual. I plead with her to calm down as the familiar words of blame are already being lobbied toward me.

"You scared me to death. Why do you do this to me?"

Despite the noise of my mother's commotion, I'm able to hear the bedroom door jerk open, followed by my grandfather's feet stomping down the hallway. I feel another wave of anxiety and dread flood through me. There will be no quick resolution to peace now.

He enters the kitchen shouting, "What in the world is going on in here?"

He aims his question accusingly toward my mother. The story spills out. Regardless, he seems unmoved, still grouchy about his disturbed sleep, having only been in bed a short while.

"Nancy, get a hold of yourself," he demands of my mother before trudging back down the hallway.

With my grandfather's declaration and huffed retreat to bed, enough space finally clears for me to interject what I have been needing to say, what ranks most important to me in that moment. With fresh rivulets of tears streaming down my cheeks, I hold up my wounded Trapper Keeper.

"It tore when I fell. Can I get a new one?"

When I revisit that vulnerable yet determined little girl running over the snowy ground, I am simultaneously looking backwards and forwards. I know things my child self can't, including that my grandfather's sudden death a few years after this incident will silence the only adult voice that ever dared speak truth to my mother. I know that for many years I will feel responsible for my mother's feelings, learning to abandon my own needs and wants in an effort to soothe and appease her. I will learn that part of the healing process will be recognizing my father's complicity, his refusal to rescue me in that moment or any other moments. A path forward will also involve confronting some of the people from that time who excused my mother as merely "overprotective" or a "worrywart," rather than helping her get the mental health treatment she desperately needed.

But most of all, I long for a time machine so that my fifty-two-year-old self can run alongside this child, shouting encouragement, letting her know she is going to be alright in this moment and in all the difficult future ones. If I could, I would put a cup of hot chocolate in her still cold hands. We would sit together on the floor in front of the hearth. I know, at this age, how much she loves sitting cross-legged as a book is read to her, so I would open the classic children's book, *The Mitten*, a beautiful adaption of a Ukrainian folktale. I believe the story of a lost mitten in the snow that becomes a gift of warmth and safety for woodland creatures will bring comfort to us both as it shows that not all snowy adventures harm us, that what is lost can be released to another life or purpose. I would like to let her know that her future will be rich with words, and music, and love, and that most of all, she will break the cycle of abuse so that her son will grow up with the security and assurance that only unconditional love can endow.

***

Dr. Kellie Brown is a violinist, conductor, music educator, and award-winning writer whose book, *The Sound of Hope: Music as Solace, Resistance and Salvation during the Holocaust and World War II* (McFarland Publishing, 2020), received one of the Choice Outstanding Academic Titles award. Her words have appeared in *Earth & Altar*, *Ekstasis*, *Psaltery & Lyre*, *Calla Press*, *The Primer*, and *Writerly*, among others. More information about her and her writing can be found at www.kelliedbrown.com.

25 | Everything is Going to be Alright by Debra Nicholson

I knew in my gut that today was the day I would leave my marriage. I spent the morning cleaning the house and preparing food for guests. I dusted to Bruce Springsteen and mopped to Billy Joel. The glass tables sparkled. My home looked spotless, and the aroma of a rustic spanakopita pie baking filled the air. I chose the wine carefully to match the leg of lamb marinating in the fridge.

This picture of domestic bliss and perfection was so far from reality that I had trouble integrating my relationship with it. I needed to get out. For the last few years, it felt like we had been trying to plug the hole in our sinking ship marriage with chewing gum.

It was time to tell my husband of thirty-five years, Flash, that I needed this marriage to be over. My entire body had been exploding with pain, and it wanted a decision. However, my mind always wanted to investigate one more counselor or one more healing modality. My body won. I could not wait any longer. I had enough information to know I could not be well in this relationship.

So, Flash and I sat in front of the large window in the living room overlooking the beautifully manicured front lawn. We were awkward and silent for a moment, and then I sensed a deep-rooted source of strength within.

It was one of those conversations where I was shaking, but inside, there was something solid and trustworthy. I felt rooted and grounded as I spoke.

Flash leaned forward.

"I love you so much, Flash. I care deeply about you. But I can't live like this. I need things to get better, and they aren't. They are getting worse. I can't live in this much pain anymore."

His body stiffened as he waited for me to say more.

"What else can I say? We have said it all before. I have decided that I want out of our marriage."

He wasn't surprised but his face tightened as he grew serious. I expected an angry reaction. Instead, he quietly said, "I am sorry that I keep hurting you. I don't know how to stop."

His heart was breaking as he told me that he had ruined everything. The gravity of the situation was evident on his face. He suddenly looked old and scared.

While kind and gracious, his response was a little disappointing. I would have liked a bit of begging or anger. Not so I would change my mind, but just so I would have the satisfaction of knowing that he was really fighting for me.

What happened next surprised me. I expected to break down and cry, but instead, I felt only relief. My body relaxed, my anxiety dissipated, and I knew I had said what I needed to say lovingly and truthfully. For the first time in months, I felt completely at ease.

My peace quickly gave way to panic as I looked at the dining room table and remembered our dinner party. The thought of bringing guests into our vulnerable space was inconceivable. So, we canceled the dinner, opened a bottle of robust wine, and spent the evening together, savoring the taste of fresh spanakopita with grilled lamb. After the first glass of wine, the somberness dissipated, and we laughed about our early relationship foibles. There was no blame, no struggle, just two friends thinking about their past together.

We never had another dinner party in that house. That was the last bottle of wine we drank together. Everything we owned was packed into boxes, including the corkscrew. We sold the house I adored and loaded my furniture into a storage container.

The day after my storage unit was loaded, I headed on a solo trip to begin my new life. I was sixty-one-years old and separated. My children were adults living on their own. I had four months off work and a file stuffed with plane tickets, Airbnb bookings, and four months of pay cheques. I had no mortgage payments, no car payments, and a job that I loved, which I planned to return to.

Sitting on the airplane headed for my first destination, London, I struggled to get comfortable. Three people with larger bodies were on this airplane, and we were all seated in one row. The lights were kept low on the plane to encourage us to sleep, but I could not rest.

Instead of sleeping, I reflected on my life. Just two years earlier, I would have told you I lucked out when I met and married my husband. Flash was my best friend. Our marriage was imperfect, but it was one of the best marriages I had seen. It had surpassed my expectations.

Then one day, everything changed.

The day began innocently enough. I headed off to work, and Flash made plans to meet up at our friend's fiftieth anniversary party. Fifty years was quite an achievement. My heart was bursting with delight as I went about my tasks that day.

We had been married for thirty-six years, and I thought about how exciting it would be to reach that milestone. I loved my husband, and I loved our life together. Of course, I knew that death or sickness could prevent us from a fiftieth wedding anniversary, but the idea of divorce or separation was unthinkable.

My phone beeped, and it was Flash. He wondered if he had left his cell phone in the car. I saw it there and told him I'd bring it to the party.

As I settled back into my work, a thought lingered in my mind about Flash and his cell phone. I was surprised he noticed his cell phone was missing; he seldom used it.

I tried to settle back into work, but there was something about Flash's phone that I could not let go of. I remembered that I had been looking for my brother's phone number in Flash's call log last week. His log differed from mine because all the phone numbers were to unknown callers. In my call log, there are almost always names beside the numbers, my son, daughter, mom, and friends.

155

So, I decided to phone some of the numbers on his call log and see who he was calling. A very troubling story started to emerge.

First call
"Hello?" answered a woman's unfamiliar voice.
"Hi, I found your phone number and can't remember what it is for."
Click.

Second Call
"Hello, can I help you?" said another unfamiliar woman's voice.
"You called me, and I am returning your call."
"What's your name?" she said.
"Debra. Who are you?"
Click.

Third call.
"Good morning, Paradise."
"Hello, what kind of business is this?"
Click.

I started googling these phone numbers, and the bottom dropped out of my world. My body felt cold and empty, like I was not there in my flesh. I viewed websites with pictures of young women offering names for sexual activities, like BBFS (bareback full service) or BFE (boyfriend experience). Flash had a whole life that I knew nothing about. It would be at least two years before I discovered its extent.

Flying over the Atlantic, I became aware that a flight attendant stood next to me. "Would you like water? Or a tissue?"

Through my tears, I replied, "Some wine would be great."

"Be right back," she said and then returned with wine, chocolate, and packages of tissues. These three very common items became the holy trifecta that helped me to grieve and to celebrate over the next few months. They became symbols of both joy and grief.

The pilot announced that we were reaching our destination, but there would be a delay, and we might have to land at an alternate airport. There was an audible groan throughout the plane.

Across the aisle, an older man hugged his traveling companion. Without any warning, tears cascaded down my cheeks. These were not the soft and quiet tears I had wept earlier. These were ugly, snotty tears that sounded like a goat screaming.

The flight attendant returned to me, thinking I was upset about the flight delay. She assured me that the airline would look after any necessary changes, and she would get help for me at the gate. I could not talk through my tears. I would have told her I did not care about the flight delay. I was not in a rush to go anywhere.

I got out my journal and wrote about the elderly couple across from me. The little jokes they shared, the way they looked deeply into one another, and the physical affection they shared were touching. It triggered intense sadness and jealousy as I realized how much I had valued my long-term relationship and how much I would miss it. I wanted to have inside jokes with someone and a comfortable way of being together. I was sad that my marriage was an illusion.

I had been living with a man that I did not know. Flash was the proverbial comfortable sweater, the crocheted blanket always lying on the couch and available. Yet, he was a stranger who could lie to me so effectively that I trusted him implicitly.

My "faithful, loyal, truthful" husband was none of those things.

Flash had repeatedly told me that he still wanted to get back together, but I sensed only pain there for me. As I sat on the plane, I desperately wanted to be a couple again. I wanted Flash to be the one squished into the seat beside me so that I could feel his warm body pressing into mine. I wanted to put my head on his chest and enjoy the safety and security I had previously felt there.

While writing in my journal, a glass of water and wine appeared on my tray table. Now the cabin crew was coming to pick up the dishes and garbage. In my journal, I quickly wrote one last thing: "Today is the beginning of my new life, and I will learn to navigate it in new ways."

I traveled through Europe and Asia for the next three months indulging my curiosity. I sampled new and exotic food and drinks. I ate simple food in a monastery. I rediscovered the joy of eating meditatively. I rediscovered the joy of community around a table with people from all over the world.

My spirituality was nurtured by food and nature and art. I experienced art slowly and purposefully in a way that filled my soul. I soaked up spiritual strength in cities and forests. Nuns, priests, monks, and healers spoke words of love and comfort to me. Traditional and non-traditional religious spaces helped me to reexamine and explore the foundation of love that my life was built on.

***

Debra Nicholson is a retired minister who lives and plays in Guelph, ON. Her network of relationships and her connections to the One Who is Love give her strength to welcome each new day.

26 | Something Is Wrong, I Know It by Johanne Pelletier

I am sitting in a small medical examination room. I am not sure where to look because the doctor is facing me, staring at the computer screen. She reviews the numbers, results from some emergency blood work done this morning. Behind the doctor are her research assistant and a nurse, both also staring at the screen. Behind them is the gynecological table I was just on.

I don't want to look at any of them too closely because maybe I will see their worry. And I want to keep myself together, composed, ready for good or bad news. I can't risk over-reading something on their faces.

They probably never react to what they see on the screen. This is, after all, a cancer center, and this clinic specializes in ovarian and endometrial cancers. Whatever they see on that screen they have seen many times before, results that are worse, or better, or maybe just like mine.

So, I fix my eyes on the handwritten notes about me in front of the doctor. Something about trying to read them upside down distracts and calms me. I see the first line, woman, fifties, extreme pelvic and back pain, started four weeks ago, morphine. That's as far as I can get, but I assume my medical history follows everything I told the doctor's assistant this morning.

The doctor stares at the screen and says, "I am not sure yet, but yes, something is wrong."

I say, "finally!" out loud with a sigh of relief. All three look at me.

I explain, "No, it's not that I want something to be wrong, but it's just that I have been in pain for weeks and finally, someone believes me. I didn't know what was wrong, but I knew something was up."

The doctor responds, "It's okay, we understand. Yes, unfortunately, this happens a lot."

Now she wants me to tell her again, from the beginning.

"My symptoms started suddenly four weeks ago. I am in excellent health, post-menopausal, no issues, but overnight I had gripping abdominal discomfort, pelvic and back pain, indigestion, bloating, and then fevers. Then there's the unexplained weight loss."

The history of navigating this health issue is very organized in my head. I can narrate my journey of pain with medical precision. I learned how to do this long ago in one of my first jobs, working as a clerk in the emergency room. I learned early what the doctors listen to and what they filter out. I know the right amount of detail, which I deliver with calm and composure.

But beneath my stealth delivery, I am a simmering mess of exhaustion, fear, and anger. Exhausted from weeks of pain and painkillers and lack of sleep. Afraid and angry about time spent bartering, campaigning, and hustling to be heard, desperate to save myself from whatever this is, desperate to be seen and taken seriously.

I continue telling the doctor about going to an emergency room one night when it felt like a knife was cutting through my pelvis. The ER doctors tested everything, and believed whatever this was, it wasn't gynecological. Although they acknowledged there was something massive in my uterus and other growths around my ovaries, they said those growths never cause pain. I wondered if they knew the feeling of period pain, of endometriosis, something I had experienced throughout my life. That heavy and piercing feeling when you know something in your gut is awry. In the emergency room, they gave me an IV with morphine to ease my pain and I felt the first relief in weeks. They were adamant all the tests showed this was not a gynecological issue.

In that small examination room, my audience, the doctor, the assistant, the nurse—everyone takes notes.

That night in the ER, desperate for a solution, I negotiated with the doctors. They said maybe it's an infection. My fear, my terror, my anger morphed into strategy and bold talk. When the doctors said they were sending me home with morphine and antibiotics, I responded, "With all due respect, why not humor me? I know you don't think anything is wrong, but this pain is real—I waited twelve hours to see you and I think there is something going on. I feel it. Nobody else is here tonight at least in this section of the emergency room, so how about giving me the antibiotics right now, stop the morphine so I will know if the pain stops, let me stay overnight, and then we'll see?"

I can't go home without an answer. The doctors nod and walk away.

I got to stay in emergency. The morphine stopped, and I got the antibiotics. I slept a little, but the pain returned, and, in the morning, they ordered me to leave. They gave me a promise of a gynecological referral to follow, a further scan of my pelvis for something on my hipbone, and a prescription for painkillers. And then I went home, still sick, but with new ideas.

I contacted a former colleague at another university. Did she know anyone in the Faculty of Medicine who could be helpful? I shared some of the story, a less personal, less detailed version. An hour later, she texted me phone numbers of clinics. This could take weeks to arrange. I make some calls.

Then I remembered another colleague, Nadia, posted on Instagram about her ovarian cancer journey. I reread her posts. And then I Googled my symptoms. Mine are like hers were months ago.

I messaged her, "Hey, I am sorry if this is inappropriate, but I am scared."

I described my symptoms. She said, "Don't apologize; we need to help each other."

Back in that small exam room, I tell the doctor, "It was Nadia, that's how I found you. Your patient Nadia connected me with your office. Thanks for squeezing me in today. I know how busy you are."

And with that sentence, everything burst out of me; a loud cry, and sobbing tears—everything so tightly held under my careful precise descriptions of symptom.

The doctor hands me Kleenex and assures me, "It's okay. You did the right thing."

She turns the computer screen toward me, pointing to the numbers from my bloodwork.

She explains, "Most of the numbers reflecting cancer markers are just barely okay. But your fever and symptoms are concerning. These cancers, ovarian cancers, are sneaky, silent, so when the symptoms appear, it's all too late."

So, all that triumph, the high and happy feeling I had about being heard, shouting finally, fades. This conversation is serious, and now it's just me here with the data, the science, and the doctor, and a vague sense that the next steps are coming.

The doctor folds her hands together on the table between us, looks at me squarely and says, "This is what I can offer you. In my view, your best bet is that we remove it all. It is the safest approach to avoid these cancers. You are past menopause. You do not need these organs now and from what I see, there is some risk. But I must tell you that a hysterectomy is major surgery—at least five hours, with at least eight weeks recovery."

I am listening. But my mind is racing to complications, blood clots, issues with anesthesia, missing work, a massive surgery, the uncertainty, and the long recovery.

She continues, "This is up to you. Maybe these symptoms will pass, maybe the numbers will right themselves. Sometimes the growths disappear on their own. Or it is an early stage of something—something more serious. We know a lot about uterine and ovarian growths, but not enough to offer a definitive assessment always. In sum, I think you are at risk and there is something wrong. But it's up to you. I wish more women would listen to their symptoms as you did. And be as persistent as you were, even when doctors told you differently."

Our eyes meet. "I don't think I can live like this. The pain in particular, but the weight of the last weeks, the uncertainty, the mad panic to get help."

Her phone rings—an emergency—she steps out to see another patient. She will be back. The assistant and nurse follow.

I get up on the examination table and close my eyes. I fall asleep, feeling the accumulated exhaustion of the last weeks, desperate to get someone to listen. And here, strangely in this tiny room, having been heard finally, I feel safe.

I wake up—it's been thirty minutes, and someone has come in and put a blanket over me. I close my eyes again and run through it all in my head.

So, I can avoid surgery and all that comes with it and hope that all this just passes. Maybe it's not cancer, but what if it is? But even if whatever it is passes with every checkup, every GYN exam, every year, I will worry. I might miss my chance to fix this if it is the start of something. What if it's a cancer that cannot be fixed or cured easily later? I have already had the hip scan from the referral in the ER—it was nothing. Should I call a friend, get a second opinion, wait for that other GYN clinic from the ER referral to contact me?

It's clear now.

I open my eyes. I am still alone here in this tiny exam room, with the crumpled Kleenex, my blood test results on the screen, and a file with my name on it. I open the file and see my ultrasound images. My uterus is distorted beyond its normal size with two massive grapefruit sized shaded images inside.

That blast of tears, the nap, being heard, it all felt good after four weeks of intense hustle. I think about my cold calls to clinics and doctors, to colleagues and friends, at every turn baring my soul and symptoms, wondering how many other women work this hard to be heard. And here I am, with the go-to specialist in gynecology oncology. And now I have the facts.

From the start, I knew it. I know my body and I knew; something was wrong—and I was right.

The doctor returns. "So, what are you thinking?"

I tell her, "I can't live without doing anything. Let's do it, take it all out."

I sign up for the surgery.

Just over five hours later, the doctor is at my side in recovery. She reports it went well. My focus now is to rest and recover. What about the possibility of cancer, I ask? They feel the surgery was necessary and they must review the removed tissue to confirm more conclusively that it is not ovarian cancer. Until then I wait and recover at home.

Four weeks later, I return to that tiny examination room, to the doctor, her assistant, the nurse, the screen of data, and my file on the desk. My bloodwork is clear, and the tissue removed revealed no cancer but there was risk of it arising had I not had the surgery. I feel tears coming but hold them in, focusing on the doctor's words. She tells me that the hysterectomy was both necessary and preventative, and how right I was to listen to my body, my symptoms, that she wished more women would do the same. She tells me about annual follow up examinations and blood tests in the future and everything she says is a blur because all I feel is relief–beyond the pain, the surgery, the waiting for results, the uncertainty.

Recovered now and pain free almost two years later, I'm glad I trusted my gut. I wish the same for all.

***

Johanne Pelletier is a storyteller and writer based in Montreal Canada where she works in communications and teaches storytelling to scientists and startups. She performs her work in Canada and the U.S., is a past winner of the GRIT 99-Second Story Grand Slam, has been featured on WGBH's *Stories from the Stage*, and is creator of *Good Gynecology*, a show about women's health stories. When not thinking about the next story, she is an amateur boxing judge. For more, see jpelletier.ca.

27 | Talking Over Ghosts by Madeline Wierzal

I used to find it so hard to talk to people, on account of the ghosts. They always insisted on having the first and final word. On first dates, I'd clam up because any time I tried to talk, the ghosts of my exes came by to snidely laugh at my fumbling attempts at romance. When I tried to come out to my friends, the spirit of my mother kept shushing and reminding me that there are things We Do Not Speak Of, not with anyone. When I tried to ask my sister why we were drifting apart, a young, teenaged apparition of her would stare at me with dead, darkened eyes and say I knew full fucking well why.

Heartache, raw from a recent breakup, was making me desperate, making me willing to try truly bizarre and unheard-of maneuvers, like talking to my sister … about romance.

I think the ghosts could also tell I was about to try something extreme, because they showed up in droves. My Sunday School CCD teacher was lurking near the old radiator, letting out an occasional, disapproving hiss. Specters of our parents lingered behind my dinged-up coffee table, with the haze of their judgement obscuring their heads like a storm cloud. The faintest hint of a couple men I'd dated, at varying levels of success, floated like mist in the corner of the living room. That angry teenaged echo of Tasha, my sister, was even there, lurking just behind the true, fully grown Tasha, who sat reclined on my living room couch next to me. Her younger shade had the crueler, dead, and shadowed eyes I remembered from that difficult part of her adolescence. Sometimes, I struggled to see that she no longer had those eyes, but plain blue ones, like mine. These older eyes looked at me now, wondering why I asked her over.

Tasha and I hadn't really spoken about dating at all before. Not talking about things was our favorite game since puberty. Our

166

second favorite game was trying to talk, then getting into shouting matches when our conversation fell too close to the war-torn grounds of touchy subjects.

Heartbroken desperation, though, was making me desperate. I made the opening gambit.

"Thanks for coming." I started.

"Yeah, no worries." She replied, deadpan.

"I mean, I'm glad you could make it. We oughta do this—hang out—more often." The couch rustled as I shifted awkwardly at these attempts at casual banter.

"Sure." My sister did not rustle. If anything, she wasn't moving at all, maybe as a prey response. Her face was unreadable. She must've wondered why I asked her here.

"I … if you don't mind, I could really use someone to talk to, about stuff we don't normally talk about. It's … I just … I'm not doing good. And I don't have anyone else I can really talk to about this stuff."

The list of friends I was comfortable talking about the breakup with was the same list of friends I would feel comfortable openly crying in front of. That list was basically non-existent, because my not being able to talk about difficult things extended well past the borders of family.

My one closest friend that topped the okay-to-cry-in-front-of list was K, the new ex in question, so she was disqualified from these conversations by default.

"What is it?" Tasha asked.

"You know K and I broke up, right?"

"Yeah. I know."

"It, well, it ended mutually. You know, we agreed to stay friends. But it … it's still hard."

"Uh-huh."

She seemed to settle into the couch as she realized what kind of "talk" I needed to have with her. Well, at least she wasn't running away, yet.

"It's just ... this ... it's probably the first serious relationship that I've not just felt, like, glad to escape."

The ghostly exes of mine that lingered faintly in the corner faded away with those words, leaving only some dancing dust motes spot-lit by the lamp on my corner end table. That was new. The living room was slightly less crowded with ghouls.

"Like I still like her, and I'm really, really, so happy we both wanted to stay friends, but ..."

Tasha blinked, waiting for me to continue. I blinked, wondering how to put into words the feelings I'd had earlier that day, laying on this very same couch and crying while listening to Patsy Cline's "She's Got You" on loop for half an hour. Could Tasha feel the dampness in those gray cushions from my earlier tears?

"I just ... I feel so bad. I couldn't make it work. This was maybe the best—or the first serious relationship I've ever had before, and I couldn't make it work."

"But you guys are staying friends?" Tasha asked.

"Yeah."

"I mean, I've never done that before, stayed friends after a breakup." Tasha ventured.

She shifted in her seat. Maybe she was haunted by her own ghosts, by something that made her willing to sit and talk this through with me.

My eyes widened at this indirect acknowledgement that she'd dated and broken up with a person, likely even people, as in multiple. This data basically doubled my knowledge of her love life. I almost didn't register that my sister was attempting to reassure me.

"Oh. Well, yeah, thanks." I answered, realizing just in time that she'd paid me something like a compliment.

I continued. "Honestly, she made it sound like the fear that I wouldn't want to be just friends is what made her hang on so long in the first place. And I was so worried about the same thing. I felt bad about being the one to bring up breaking up, and then also bad that I hadn't done it sooner." I went on, warming up as Tasha showed she was willing to talk about this.

"How long did you two date?" She asked.

"Um, about a year. Kinda." I answered.

"Kinda?"

"Well, I think it's one of those things where I sort of thought of us as a thing for way sooner than she did. So, like, by my count it'd been over a year. But I think by her count it was a bit less. I was always the one to really move these things along, to talk to her about this stuff. Relationship stuff. And now I'm the one that ended it."

That last sentence twisted my throat tight, with the threat of tears.

"So, you guys weren't on the same page about when you started dating, and you were the one that usually had to get her started talking about, uh, relationship stuff. And she'd also been thinking about breaking up, but didn't say anything until you did?"

"Yes." I crumpled under this answer, my arms crossing to hold myself together.

Tasha summed it all up perfectly. I was a terrible person, unworthy and incapable of love, nagging my girlfriend until she left me forever. Tasha's own cruel ghost loved to remind me of this, every night, indulging that old sniping temper.

"Well, it sounds like maybe she wasn't that great at communicating with you. Do you think that's fair to say?" Tasha tilted her head forward with this hypothesis.

What?

She caught me so off guard I forgot to say "what" out loud. The angry eyed little shade of my teenaged sister fizzled away from her

169

side into nothing but the smell of burnt coal, and a singe mark on the arm of my couch.

"I guess, yeah. I see what you mean. She kinda could, uh, withdraw sometimes."

"I can see how that'd make handling a relationship so hard."

"Yeah …" I trailed off.

How did she do that? Make this sound so normal? Make neither me nor K sound like any sort of villain or failure? We were just trying to do something hard, and we just decided to do something different to make both of us happier.

"And I mean, on top of everything, she was your first girlfriend, right? You'd never been in a relationship with a woman before? Or been open about being asexual?"

"Yeah. Yeah, I'd never been able to talk about all that with a partner before."

A panicked buzz came from the Catholic cloud of judgement and repression that engulfed our parents' ghosts. The buzz grew so load the coasters and loose knick-knacks on my coffee table started to vibrate with them. My CCD teacher's eyes flared up with a ghostly glint of hellfire. I wouldn't give up though, not with two ghosts already down. I pressed on.

Tasha continued. "Have you considered then that you might be putting too much stock on the idea of this relationship because of all that? Like, this is the first time you've been able to be authentic in a relationship, and you can't imagine how you'd be able to do it again?" She eyed me to see how I'd take her words.

How was she able to take things that sounded so scary bouncing around in my head at 3 a.m., and make them sound so simple, so matter of fact?

"Maybe. Yeah, that could be it."

I acknowledged her insight and attempted to start processing it. I could almost hear my brain's exhaust fan turn on as my wheels spun, overheating.

Having someone know me better than myself seriously fatigued me. I had to figure out how we could pivot to another topic, naturally.

"So ... um ... I know you probably have more experience than me at, ah, dating. How do you handle breakups? How do you get over them?"

"Oh yeah, I've had plenty of breakups. I don't know that I had any sort of strategy that made them less hard. I think usually I just kept going through people, 'til I burned out on the whole dating thing for a while. I mean, whatever gave you the whole asexual deal probably turned the dial all the way in the other direction for me, libido wise." She tsk-ed a small laugh at herself.

"Right, so you really like the physical stuff, with men and ... and women then?" I asked, off a very calculated suspicion.

"Oh yeah, sure, boys, girls, gender never really meant a thing to me." At her answer, I silently and internally fist pumped to myself that my math was, for once, solid.

Hearing Tasha's revelation, the specter of our parents popped into nothing but a shock of white smoke. Did my sister blink at them, just then? My old CCD teacher, who'd been sneering in distaste throughout this whole thing, finally shrank away at her admission with one last hiss of "Itssss Adam and Eeeeeve, not Adam and Steeeeeve ..." I ignored those ghosts making dramatic exits and just eagerly nodded at my sister to continue.

"I mean really, what I always have a hard time with, is, like, finding someone I actually want to keep around. And of course, I really need to work on my standards ..." She said, more than ready to go on about her romantic troubles, now that I'd gotten us started.

We continued, the conversational tide pulling away from the precious little stones of revelation left at my feet, and on to my sister's own problems, how sick she was of online dating, what a goober this one guy was on her last date, how quickly this one girl asked to move in with her, and so on. Her stories, her troubles, were wild and different from my own, but incredibly reassuring in that they were there, and we were both willing to talk about them, and keep talking about them, with no malicious ghosts looming over us.

Words of truth from the ones we love, it turns out, are the most effective exorcism you could ever hope for. All my ghosts lay dead and quiet.

***

Madeline Wierzal is a writer and poet from Evanston Illinois. Born and raised by bibliophiles in the suburbs of Chicago, she started writing from a young age. As she grew, she found new ways to share her stories. Eventually, she had her writing published in several publications, including *After Hours*, *Ephimiliar Journal*, *AZE Journal*, and *Popshot Quarterly*. She also shares work on her own personal blog, maddwierdpoetry.com.

About the Editor | Anne E. Beall, PhD

Anne E. Beall is an award-winning author whose books have been featured in *People Magazine, Chicago Tribune, Toronto Sun, Hers Magazine, Ms. Career Girl,* and she's been interviewed by NBC, NPR, and WGN. Her book, *Cinderella Didn't Live Happily Ever After: The Hidden Messages in Fairy Tales* won a Gold award from Literary Titan. Her sequel, *Only Prince Charming Gets to Break the Rules,* won a Silver award from Literary Titan. And her *Heartfelt Connections* book was named one of the top 100 Notable Indie books in 2016 by *Shelf Unbound.* She has published in several literary journals including *Minerva Rising Press, The Raven's Perch, You Might Need to Hear This,* and *Grande Dame Literary Journal.* She received her PhD in social psychology from Yale University and is the founder of the strategic market-research firm, Beall Research.

About the Editor | Judi Lee Goshen

Judi is a writer, actor, and storyteller. Her *book Fornicationally Challenged: My Reluctant Return to Dating*, received a Readers' Favorite Award as well as one of the Top 100 Notable Books by *Shelf Unbound*. She has been published in *Beyond Words Literary Magazine*, *The South Loop Review*, and *Story Salon*. Several of her screenplays and teleplays have garnered recognition from *Writer's Digest* and The Slamdance Competitions.

As a Moth winning storyteller, Judi has written and told hundreds of stories including her comedic one-woman show, *Fornicationally Challenged*, which was directed by Mark Travis.

Her free time, and her heart, belong to her two grandchildren.

Acknowledgements

This book would not be possible without the talented collection of storytellers who submitted their stories. These authors make this book funny, heartwarming, and meaningful. It was a pleasure to work with all of you.

We are grateful that you have shared a part of yourself through your story: Liza Anderson, Wendy Banks, Barbara Apelian Beall, Sherrill Bodine, Kellie D. Brown, Tracey Croisier, Raine Grayson, John Hahm, Madeleine Holden, Toneal M. Jackson, Jeannine Kacmar, Faith R. Kares, Sky Khan, Avesha Michael, Debra Nicholson, P.A. O'Neil, Johanne Pelletier, Lee Roscoe, Gavin Ross, Andrew Shelffo, Elizabeth Smiley, Nina Smith, LaVern Spencer McCarthy, Linda Strader, Anne Wagner, Madeline Wierzal. Your stories made us laugh, cry, and above all, think differently about the world in which we live.

We also want to thank the talented Atiq Ahmed who created the cover for this book. Your design captured the feeling of triumph.

And thank you, reader, for picking up this volume.

Thank you and Feedback

Dear Reader,

Thank you so much for spending your time reading this book. We hope that you enjoyed these stories and found the tellers inspiring.

If you have feedback about the book, you can email us at ChicagoStoryPress@gmail.com. Whether you loved it or hated it, tell us what you think.

Finally, if you have a few minutes, it will help tremendously if you would write a quick review on Amazon.

Reviews make an enormous difference, and the more reviews a book receives, the more people will learn about it.

Thanks again,

Anne E. Beall & Judi Lee Goshen

Made in the USA
Monee, IL
08 December 2023

47623306R00106